KNITTED FAIRY TALES

Delightful and Enchanting Characters to Make

Cilla Webb

CONTENTS

Introduction 4
    The Essentials 5
    Abbreviations 5
Glossary of How To's 6

Projects **13**
Dragon 14
The Frog Prince 22
Genie in the Lamp 26
Noble Steed 32
Knight 38
Merlin 44
Mermaid 50
Ogre 58
Princess 62
Puss in Boots 68
Dwarf 74
Troll 78
Wand 84
Witch 88
Woodland Faeries 96

Acknowledgements 102

NTRODUCTION

This book started with one cheeky little fairy called Lilly. Whenever something got misplaced in my classroom, I used to tell my pupils that the fairies must have taken it. One day they decided to build a fairy trap out of a cardboard box for this mischievous little creature. We left the trap in the class room on Friday and on Monday a cheeky little knitted fairy appeared inside. The children in my class were amazed and it prompted me to start working on other fairy tale characters. I started with a mermaid (because who doesn't love a mermaid?) and a not so wicked witch. Soon all the other characters quickly followed suit. They were a huge hit with my two little boys and they loved enacting fairy tales and creating their own version along the way.

THE ESSENTIALS

Yarn

All the characters featured in this book have been knitted using Wendy Merino DK wool, which is soft, durable and most importantly washable! When choosing the yarn for your creations, you can opt to go for a lighter or heavier yarn weight, however keep in mind that this will make your critter smaller or bigger than in the picture.

Needles

All my creatures have been knitted using 3.5mm (US 4) straight needles, which is 2 sizes smaller than suggested on the yarn band. This allows for the finished fabric to be nice and tight, which will prevent the stuffing from showing through.

Stuffing

As with the yarn, choose a stuffing that is washable and suitable for soft toys.

Accessories

A tapestry needle, a sewing needle, a crochet hook for some of the hair styles and scissors.

ABBREVIATIONS

[ ] x times: Knit the instructions between the brackets x amount of times.

* ; rep from * to end: Repeat the instructions between the * and ; until the end of the row.

MC: Main color.

CC: Contrast color st(s): stitch(es).

K: knit, if followed by a number, knit that amount of stitches.

P: purl.

St st: stocking stitch: alternate a row of knitting and a row of purling.

G st: garter stitch: knit every row.

K2tog: knit two stitches together knitwise.

P2tog: purl two stitches together purlwise.

Kfb: knit in the front and back of the stitch, creating an increase.

Pfb: Purl in the front and back of the stitch, creating an increase.

sl1: Slip one stitch to the right hand needle

psso: Pass slipped stitch over.

Ssk: Slip 1, slip 1, knit these two slipped stitches together through the back, creating a decrease.

Yo: yarn over: wrap the yarn over the right needle.

 LOSSARY OF HOW TO'S

SAFETY FIRST

I try not to add any plastic eyes and noses to my creatures as I have two small boys myself and will only add buttons when I know the toy will not belong to a little chewer. If you do choose to add these, please ensure that all parts are securely attached and that your knitted fabric has a nice tight gauge so little people cannot pull the stuffing out.

SEWING UP

For a clean edge I prefer to use the mattress stitch when sewing finished pieces together. To join two pieces vertically place both your pieces side by side next to each other with the right side facing up. Insert your tapestry needles under the horizontal bar between the first two stitches on the left side and repeat on the right. Continue going back and forth until you've worked your way up to the top. Pull the yarn tight and watch the seam disappear as if by magic! When joining two pieces horizontally (e.g. the cast-on or cast-off edge) insert the needle under the V point of the first stitch on one side and repeat on the other side. Work all the way across the seam and pull the yarn tight.

CASTING ON

There are many different ways of casting on yarn; however, when it comes to toy knitting, I find the cable cast on gives an attractive and even edge. Here's how to do it:

» Start by making a slip knot on the left-hand needle.
» Place the right-hand needle behind the first stitch and loop the yarn around it. Pull the loop over and onto the left-hand needle.
» Now insert the needle between the first and second stitch and loop the yarn over.
» Pull the next stitch onto the left-hand needle and repeat.

CAST OFF (BIND OFF)

Once you've reached the desired number of rows it's time to cast off. To do this, knit (or purl if you're on the wrong side of your work) the first two stitches, then insert the left-hand needle into the first stitch on the right-hand needle and pull this stitch up and over the second stitch you just knitted (or purled). Knit (or purl) the next stitch and repeat this process until only one stitch remains. Cut the yarn and draw the yarn end through the last stitch and fasten tightly.

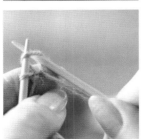

KNITTING

Starting with your stitches on the left-hand needle and the yarn behind the work, insert the tip of the right-hand needle in the front of the first stitch. Wrap the yarn around your needle counter clockwise and pull the loop through the first stitch, sliding the worked stitch off the left-hand needle and on to the right-hand one. Repeat this until all the stitches are on the right-hand needle. Swap the needles over and repeat. For a clean edge, simply slide the first stitch onto the right-hand needle without actually knitting it, then knit all the stitches to the end of the row.

PURLING

This time start with the yarn in front, bring the tip of the right-hand needle through the back of the first stitch. Wrap the yarn counter clockwise around the tip of the needle and pull the loop through the back of the stitch. Slide the worked stitch off the left-hand needle and repeat. As with the knitted stitches, simply slide the first stitch onto the right-hand needle without purling it for a sharp edge.

 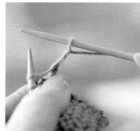  

KFB (KNIT IN FRONT AND BACK OF THE STITCH)

This stitch will allow you to increase your stitch count by one. To do this knit the stitch but do not slip the worked stitch off the left-hand needle. Instead, insert the tip of the right knitting needle behind the left knitting needle and through the back of the same stitch. Knit the stitch again in the back and then slip the worked stitch off the needle. You should now have two stitches instead of one.

K2TOG (KNIT TWO STITCHES TOGETHER)

This stitch will decrease your stitch count by one. To do this insert the tip of the right-hand needle through the next two stitches on the left knitting needle as if to knit. Work with these stitches as if they are one and knit as usual through the front loop of both at the same time.

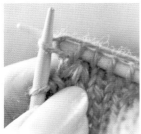

PFB (PURL IN FRONT AND BACK OF THE STITCH)

As with KFB, however this time you're increasing on the purl side. Purl the stitch but do not slide the stitch from the left-hand needle. Instead, insert the tip of the right-hand needle in the back of the worked stitch and purl again. Slip the worked stitch off the left-hand needle.

P2TOG (PURL TWO STITCHES TOGETHER)

This stitch creates a decrease. Insert the tip of the right-hand needle through the front of the next two stitches on the left-hand needle at the same time and purl them together as if they are one stitch.

BLOCKING

Sometimes when you've knitted a piece you might find it curls up slightly or, if it has eyelets, it might look scrunched up. Don't despair, there's a very simple solution to this. You must block your knitting. To do this you must pin the piece on a flat surface (I prefer to use the ironing board) and then either steam it gently (but ONLY if you're using acrylic) or make the fabric wet (if using wool). Every yarn is different and blocking instructions are often stated on the yarn band so make sure you follow them accurately.

WEAVING IN LOOSE ENDS

Once you've blocked your piece it's time to get rid of those loose yarn ends. Use a tapestry needle to weave each strand through four or five stitches on the back of the work and then cut the left over yarn.

CHANGING COLOR

To change color, simply start your row as you would normally. Insert your right-hand needle into the first stitch of the left-hand needle and wrap the first color around. Then also loop your new color around the needle and knit your first stitch. For the second stitch, insert your needle into the stitch, but this time only use the new color to knit by wrapping the yarn and the tail end around the needle and knit. Repeat this last step twice more to ensure the yarn is secured.

STRANDED KNITTING

For a few of these projects you'll need to master stranded knitting. Don't worry, it's not as hard as it seems. You simply follow the chart and add new colors when needed. However, you do have to make sure that you carry both (or more) yarns along until you reach the end of your row or pattern. You do this so that you can use them whenever you need them. To make sure your strands of yarn that have been carried along the back don't get too long twist them with your main yarn color every four stitches. Try not to twist them in the same place on every row or you'll end up with a noticeable line in your knitted fabric. Also try to remember... it's always better to have slightly loose threads floating across the back of the work than tight ones.

I-CORD

An i-cord is something I used to make as a child using a spool knitting tool (my mother called it a *tricotin* in French and my one was shaped as a purple caterpillar!). To create an i-cord you can either use one of those little tools or simply pick up two of your dpns (double pointed needles) and cast on the required number of stitches. Knit the first row and at the end do not turn the work over. Instead slide the stitches to the other end of the needles and knit a second row, bringing the yarn behind the work to start the first stitch. Try to pull the yarn as tight as possible in the beginning of the row to even out the tension. Repeat these steps until the desired number of rows has been achieved. To cast off an i-cord, break yarn and thread through remaining stitches. Pull tight and weave in any loose ends.

DRAGON

Dragons likes to spend their days in solitude, roasting prime cuts of meat over a DIY camp fire and comtemplating life. Every once in a while they do get bored and nothing beats the endless solitude than to scare a few knights and abduct a fair maiden or two. After all... what good is it being a dragon if you can't fly on the wild side of life every once in a while?

YARN USED

» 100 g (3½ oz) Wendy Merino DK Apple Green

» 50 g (2 oz) Wendy Merino Crepe

» A small amount of Birch (beige) and Jet (Black) for the eyes.

NEEDLES USED

» 3.5mm (US 4) straight needles

» 2, 3.5mm (US 4) double pointed needles

OTHER SUPPLIES

» Tapestry needle

» Stuffing

» Crochet hook for the eyes

» Scissors

INSTRUCTIONS

Dragon Head:

Cast on 10 sts in Apple Green

Row 1: [Kfb] 10 times. 20 sts

Row 2 and all even rows: P.

Row 3: [K1, kfb] 10 times. 30 sts

Row 5: [K1, kfb, k1] 10 times. 40 sts

Row 7: [K2. Kfb, k1] 10 times. 50 sts

Row 9: [K2, kfb, k2] 10 times. 60 sts

Row 10-12: St st 3 rows.

Row 13: [K3, kfb, k2] 10 times. 70 sts

Row 14-32: St st 19 rows.

Row 33: [K3, k2tog, k2] 10 times. 60 sts

Row 34-36: St st 3 rows.

Row 37: [K2, k2tog, k2] 10 times. 50 sts

Row 38-40: St st 3 rows.

Row 41: [K2, k2tog, k1] 10 times. 40 sts

Row 42-44: St st 3 rows.

Row 45: [K1, k2tog, k1] 10 times. 30 sts

Row 46-48: St st 3 rows.

Row 49: [K2tog, k1] 10 times. 20 sts

Row 51: [K2tog] 10 times. 10 sts

Break yarn and thread through rem. sts.

Pull tight and fasten. Using mattress stitch sew along the side edge and stuff. Leave the cast on edge open for adding facial features.

Body back:

Using Apple Green cast on 16 sts.

Row 1 and all odd rows: P.

Row 2: [Kfb, k1] 8 times. 24 sts

Row 3-5: St st 3 rows.

Row 6: [K1, kfb, k1] 8 times. 32 sts

Row 7-9: St st 3 rows.

Row 10: [K2, kfb, k1] 8 times. 40 sts

Row 11-15: St st 5 rows.

Row 16: [K2, kfb, k2] 8 times. 48 sts

Row 17-21: St st 5 rows.

Row 22: [K3, kfb, k2] 8 times. 56 sts

Row 23-43: St st 21 rows.

Row 44: [K3, k2tog, k2] 8 times. 48 sts

Row 46: [K2, k2tog, k2] 8 times. 40 sts

Row 48: [K2, k2tog, k1] 8 times. 32 sts

Row 50: [K1, k2tog, k1] 8 times. 24 sts

Row 52: [K1, k2tog,] 8 times. 16 sts

Row 54: [K2tog] 8 times. 8 sts

Break yarn and thread through rem. sts.

Pull tight and fasten. Set the body aside until the front of the body has been knitted.

Body front:

Using Crepe cast on 8 sts.

Row 1: P.

Row 2: [Pfb, p1] 4 times. 12 sts

Row 3-5: St st 3 rows, starting with a k row.

Row 6: [K1, kfb, k1] 4 times. 16 sts

Row 7-9: St st 3 rows, starting with a k row.

Row 10: [K2, kfb, k1] 4 times. 20 sts

Row 11-15: St st 5 rows, starting with a k row.

Row 16: [K2, kfb, k2] 4 times. 24 sts

Row 17-21: St st 5 rows, starting with a k row.

Row 22: [K3, kfb, k2] 4 times. 28 sts

Row 23–27: St st 5 rows, starting with a k row.

Row 28: K.

Row 29–33: St st 5 rows, starting with a k row.

Row 34: K.

Row 35–39: St st 5 rows, starting with a k row.

Row 40: K.

Row 41–43: St st 3 rows, starting with a k row.

Row 44: [P3, p2tog, p2] 4 times. 24 sts

Row 45: K.

Row 46: [K2, k2tog, k2] 4 times. 20 sts

Row 47: K.

Row 48: [P2, p2tog, p1] 4 times. 16 sts

Row 49: K.

Row 50: [P1, p2tog, p1] 4 times. 12 sts

Row 51: K.

Row 52: [K1, k2tog,] 4 times. 8 sts

Row 53: K.

Row 54: [P2tog] 4 times. 4 sts

Break yarn and thread through rem. sts.

Pull tight and fasten. Using mattress st attach the belly to the center of the body and stuff. Attach the cast on edge to head.

Arms: (make two)

Using Apple Green cast on 12 sts.

Row 1: P.

Row 2: Cast on 3 sts, k to end. 15 sts

Row 3: Cast on 3 sts, p to end. 18 sts

Row 4–23: St st 20 rows.

Row 24: [K2tog] 9 times. 9 sts

Break yarn and thread through rem sts.

Pull tight and fasten. Using mattress stitch sew along the side edge and stuff. Secure to either side of the body.

Nostrils: (make two)

Cast on 6 sts using Apple Green.

Row 1: [K1, kfb] 3 times. 9 sts

Row 2 and all even rows: P.

Row 3: [K1, kfb, k1] 3 times. 12 sts

Row 5: [K1, kfb, k2] 3 times. 15 sts

Row 6–8: St st 3 rows.

Row 9: [K1, k2tog, k2] 3 times. 12 sts

Row 11: [K1, k2tog, k1] 3 times. 9 sts

Row 13: [K1, k2tog] 3 times. 6 sts

Cast off.

Fold your knitting in half and sew across the edge. Attach the cast on edge to the head in a V shape.

Ears: (make two)

Cast on 16 sts in Apple Green.

Row 1: K1, kfb, k4, kfb, k2, kfb, k4, kfb, k1. 20 sts

Row 2 and all even rows: P.

Row 3: K1, kfb, k6, kfb, k2, kfb, k6, kfb, k1. 24 sts

Row 5: K1, kfb, k8, kfb, k2, kfb, k8, kfb, k1. 28 sts

Row 6–8: St st 3 rows.

Row 9: K1, k2tog, k8, k2tog, k2, k2tog, k8, k2tog, k1. 24 sts

Row 10–12: St st 3 rows.

Row 13: K1, k2tog, k6, k2tog, k2, k2tog, k6, k2tog, k1. 20 sts

Row 15: K1, k2tog, k4, k2tog, k2, k2tog, k4, k2tog, k1. 16 sts

Row 17: K1, [k2tog, k2] 3 times, k2tog, k1. 12 sts

Row 19: K1, [k2tog] twice, k2, [k2tog] twice, k1. 8 sts

Row 21: [K1, k2tog, k1] twice. 6 sts

Row 23: K1, [k2tog] twice, k1. 4 sts

Break yarn and thread through rem. sts. Pull tight and fasten.

   Fold the ears sideways and sew along the edge. There is no need to stuff the ears unless otherwise desired. Slightly pinch the side edge together and secure to the head.

Eyes: (make two)

Cast on 6 sts in Birch.

Row 1–2: St st 2 rows.

Row 3: K1, kfb, k2, kfb, k1. 8 sts

Row 4–6: St st 3 rows.

Row 7: K1, k2tog, k2, k2tog, k1. 6 sts

Cast off.

Using black yarn sew a pupil on the eye and then attach the eye on the head. Rinse and repeat.

Legs: (make two)

Using Apple Green cast on 24 sts.

Row 1–8: St st 8 rows, starting with a k row.

Row 9: [K1, kfb, k2] 6 times. 30 sts

Row 10 and all even rows: P.

Row 11: [K2, kfb, k2] 6 times. 36 sts

Row 13: [K2, kfb, k3] 6 times. 42 sts

Row 14–20: St st 7 rows.

Row 21: [K2, k2tog, k3] 6 times. 36 sts

Row 23: [K2, k2tog, k2] 6 times. 30 sts

Row 25: [K1, k2tog, k2] 6 times. 24 sts

Row 27: [K1, k2tog, k1] 6 times. 18 sts

Row 28: [P2tog, p1] 6 times. 12 sts

Break yarn and thread through rem. sts.

   Using mattress sts sew along the side edge and stuff.

Feet: (make two)

Using Apple Green cast on 24 sts.

Row 1–2: St st 2 rows, starting with a k row.

Row 3: Kfb, k12, kfb, change to crepe, kfb, k8 kfb. 28 sts

Row 4 and every even row: P, working every Apple Green st Apple Green and every crepe st crepe.

Row 5: Kfb, k14, kfb, change to crepe, kfb, k10 kfb. 32 sts

Row 7: Kfb, k16 kfb, change to crepe, kfb, k12 kfb. 36 sts

Row 8–10: St st 3 rows.

Row 11: Kfb, k18, kfb, change to crepe, kfb, k14 kfb. 40 sts

Row 12–16: St st 5 rows.

Row 17: Kfb, k20, kfb, change to crepe, kfb, k16 kfb. 44 sts

Row 18: Cast off 20 sts, P to end in Apple Green. 24 sts

Row 19: Working on the first 8 sts only: cast on 8 sts, k8. 16 sts

Row 20–24: St st 5 rows, starting with a P row.

Row 25: [k2tog] 8 times. 8 sts

Break yarn and thread through rem sts.
Pull tight and fasten.
Pick up the next 8 sts and repeat rows 19–25 twice.
Sew along the side edge and stuff. Attach the top part of the foot to the open cast on edge of the leg and then secure to the body.

Wings: (make two)

Using Apple Green cast on 14 sts

Row 1 and all odd rows: K. This is the RS and all color changes should be carried on the back.

Row 2: [Kfb in Apple Green, p1 in Crepe] 3 times, kfb in Apple Green, [Kfb in Apple Green, p1 in Crepe] 3 times, kfb in Apple Green. 22 sts

From here on work all sts in the color they are on the LH needle.

Row 4: [K1, kfb, p1] 3 times, k1, kfb, [K1, kfb, p1] 3 times, k1, kfb. 30 sts

Row 6: [K1, kfb, k1, p1] 3 times, k1, kfb, k1, [K1, kfb, k1, p1] 3 times, k1, kfb, k1. 38 sts

Row 8: [K2, kfb, k1, p1] 3 times, k2, kfb, k1, [K2, kfb, k1, p1] 3 times, k2, kfb, k1. 46 sts

Row 10: [K2, kfb, k2, p1] 3 times, k2, kfb, k2, [K2, kfb, k2, p1] 3 times, k2, kfb, k2. 54 sts

Row 12: [K6, p1] 3 times, k6, [K6, p1] 3 times, k6.

Row 13: K.

Cast off.

For the edge of the wing cast on 6 sts on dpns in Crepe. Work an i-cord of 35 rows. Break yarn and thread through rem sts.

Fold the wing in half so that both side edges meet and secure the cast on edge, side edge and the cast off edge using running sts. Next, secure the i-cord to the folded part of the wing first and then sew along the cast on edge and the side edge. Then secure the tip of the i-cord to the dragon's back.

Tail:

Using Apple Green cast on 48 sts

Row 1–4: St st 4 rows.

Row 5: [K5, k2tog, k5] 4 times. 44 sts

Row 6–10: St st 5 rows.

Row 11: [K4, k2tog, k5] 4 times. 40 sts

Row 12–16: St st 5 rows.

Row 17: [K4, k2tog, k4] 4 times. 36 sts

Row 18–22: St st 5 rows.

Row 23: [K3, k2tog, k4] 4 times. 32 sts

Row 24–28: St st 5 rows.

Row 29: [K3, k2tog, k3] 4 times. 28 sts

Row 30–34: St st 5 rows.

Row 35: [K2, k2tog, k3] 4 times. 24 sts

Row 36–40: St st 5 rows.

Row 41: [K2, k2tog, k2] 4 times. 20 sts

Row 42–46: St st 5 rows.

Row 47: [K1, k2tog, k2] 4 times. 16 sts

Row 48–52: St st 5 rows.

Row 53: [K1, k2tog, k1] 4 times. 12 sts

Row 54–58: St st 5 rows.

Row 59: [K2tog, k1] 4 times. 8 sts

Row 60–64: St st 5 rows.

Row 65: [K2tog] 4 times. 4 sts

Break yarn and thread through rem. sts. Pull tight and fasten. Sew along the side edge using mattress stitch and stuff. Attach to the lower back of the dragon.

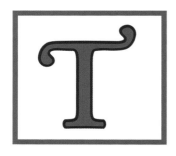 HE FROG PRINCE

Some say you have to kiss a lot of frogs before you find your handsome prince. This snuggly blanket was inspired by the fairy tale of the Frog Prince, a handsome young man who got turned into a frog by a wicked witch and only true love's kiss will transform him back to his true self.

YARN USED

» Wendy Merino DK

» 100 g (3½ oz) Wendy Merino DK Apple Green

» 10 g (½ oz) Wendy Merino DK Crepe

» Scrap amounts of Jet (black) and Birch (beige)

NEEDLES USED

» 3.5mm (US 4) straight needles

OTHER SUPPLIES

» Tapestry needle

» Stuffing

» Crochet hook for the eyes

» Scissors

SPECIAL INSTRUCTIONS

MK (Make knot): Purl 3 together, leaving them on the left needle. Knit same 3 together, and Purl same 3 together again before dropping from left needle. This does not decrease or increase the stitch count.

INSTRUCTIONS

Blanket:

Using Apple Green cast on 85 sts

Row 1: K.

Row 2: P.

Row 3: Cast off 10 sts (which leaves you with 1 st on the right hand needle), *mk, k3; rep. from * to last 14 sts, mk, k to end. 75 sts

Row 4: Cast off 10 sts, p to end. 65 sts

Row 5: K.

Row 6: P.

Row 7: K4, *mk, k3; rep. from * to last sts, k1.

Row 8: P.

Row 9: K.

Row 10 and all even rows: P.

Row 11: K1, *mk, k3; rep. from * to last 4 sts, mk, k to end.

Row 12–14: St st 3 rows, starting with a p row.

Row 15: K4, *mk, k3; rep. from * to last sts, k1.

Row 16: P.

Row 17–80: Repeat rows 9–18.

Row 81: Cast on 10 sts, k to end. 75 sts

Row 82: Cast on and 10 sts, p to end. 85 sts Cast off. Weave in any loose ends and block. Tie a knot in each corner.

Head:

Using Apple Green cast on 8 sts.

Row 1: [Kfb] 8 times. 16 sts

Row 2 and all even rows: P.

Row 3: [K1, kfb] 8 times. 24 sts

Row 5: [K1, kfb, k1] 8 times. 32 sts

Row 7: [K2, kfb, k1] 8 times. 40 sts

Row 8–26: St st 19 rows.

Row 27: [K2, k2tog, k1] 4 times and turn, leaving the rem. 20 sts waiting. 16 sts

Row 29: [K1, k2tog, k1] 4 times. 12 sts

Row 31: [K1, k2tog] 4 times. 8 sts

Row 32: [P2tog] 4 times. 4 sts

Break yarn and thread through rem. Sts. Pull tight and fasten. Repeat rows 27–32 with the 20 sts waiting. Using mattress st sew along the side edge and stuff.

Crown:

Using Crepe cast on 21 sts.

Row 1–4: St st 4 rows.

Row 5: K1, [yo, k2tog] 10 times. 21 sts

Row 6–10: St st 5 rows.

Cast off. Fold the cast on and cast off edge towards each other and secure using running sts. Sew along the side edge and secure onto the head of the frog.

Using a small amount of black, crochet a chain of 6 sts and join in the round with a slip st. Make another and attach to the frog's head as the eyes. Using a small amount of beige sew 2 stitches in each pupil. Attach the frog's head to the center of the blanket.

GENIE IN THE LAMP

In an exotic land, far away, there is a tale about a magical lamp. Inside this lamp resides a powerful genie who will grant the holder of the lamp three wishes. However, be careful what you wish for as these genies have a wicked sense of humor...

YARN USED

- » Wendy Merino DK; 116m (380 ft) per 50 g (2 oz) ball; 100% Merino wool
- » 50 g (2 oz) Wendy Merino DK Crepe
- » 25 g (¾ oz) Wendy Merino DK Latte
- » 25 g (¾ oz) Wendy Merino DK Seaspray

NEEDLES USED

- » 3.5mm (US 4) straight needles
- » 2, 3.5mm (US 4) double pointed needles

OTHER SUPPLIES

- » Tapestry needle
- » Stuffing
- » Crochet hook

INSTRUCTIONS

Lamp:

Using Crepe cast on 16 sts.

Row 1 and all odd rows: P.

Row 2: [Kfb, k1] 8 times. 24 sts

Row 4: [K1, kfb, k1] 8 times. 32 sts

Row 6: [k1, kfb, k2] 8 times. 40 sts

Row 8: [K2, kfb, k2] 8 times. 48 sts

Row 10: [K2, kfb, k3] 8 times. 56 sts

Row 12: [K3, kfb, k3] 8 times. 64 sts

Row 13–27: st st 15 rows.

Row 28: [K3, k2tog, k3] 8 times. 56 sts

Row 30: [K2, k2tog, k3] 8 times. 48 sts

Row 32: [K2, k2tog, k2] 8 times. 40 sts

Row 34: [K1, k2tog, k2] 8 times. 32 sts

Row 36: [K1, k2tog, k1] 8 times. 24 sts

Row 38: [K1, kfb, k1] 8 times. 32 sts

Row 40: [k1, kfb, k2] 8 times. 40 sts

Row 42: [K2, kfb, k2] 8 times. 48 sts

Row 44: [K2, kfb, k3] 8 times. 56 sts

Row 46: [K3, kfb, k3] 8 times. 64 sts

Row 47–61: st st 15 rows.

Row 62: [K3, k2tog, k3] 8 times. 56 sts

Row 64: [K2, k2tog, k3] 8 times. 48 sts

Row 66: [K2, k2tog, k2] 8 times. 40 sts

Row 68: [K1, k2tog, k2] 8 times. 32 sts

Row 70: [K1, k2tog, k1] 8 times. 24 sts

Row 72: [K2tog, k1] 8 times. 16 sts

Row 74: [K2tog] 8 times. 8 sts

Break yarn and thread through rem. sts. Pull tight and fasten. Sew along the side edge using mattress st and fold the cast on edge towards the center to create a bowl shape.

Base:

Using Crepe create an i-cord of 6 sts measuring 12 cm (4½ in) long. Join the i-cord in a circle using mattress st and secure to the bottom of the lamp.

Handle:

Using Crepe create an i-cord of 6 sts measuring 12 cm (4½ in) long. Attach to one side of the lamp.

Spout:

Using Crepe cast on 18 sts.

Row 1–4: St st 4 rows starting with a k row.

Row 5: K16, turn, p14, turn, k12, turn, p10, turn, k8, turn, p10, turn, k12, turn, p14, turn, k18.

Row 6: P.

Row 7: K2tog, k to last 2 sts, k2tog. 16 sts

Row 8: P.

Row 9-14: Repeat rows 7-8.

Row 15–16: P 2 rows.

Row 17: [K2tog] 5 times. 5 sts

Break yarn and thread through rem. sts. Pull tight and fasten. Using mattress st sew along the side edge and stuff. Attach to the front of the lamp.

Lid:

Using Crepe cast on 8 sts.

Row 1: [Kfb] 8 times. 16 sts.

Row 2 and all even rows: P.

Row 3: [K1, kfb] 8 times. 24 sts

Row 5: [K1, kfb, k1] 8 times. 32 sts

Row 7: [K2, kfb, k1] 8 times. 40 sts

Row 8–10: St st 3 rows.

Row 11: [K2, k2tog, k1] 8 times. 32 sts

Row 13: [K1, k2tog, k1] 8 times. 24 sts

Row 15: [K1, k2tog] 8 times.16 sts

Row 16: [P2tog] 8 times. 8 sts

Row 17: [Kfb] 8 times. 16 sts

Row 18–20: St st 3 rows.

Row 21: [K2tog] 8 times. 8 sts

Break yarn and thread through rem. sts. Pull tight and fasten. Using mattress st sew along the side edge.

Genie:

Using Latte cast on 16 sts

Row 1: [K1, kfb] 8 times. 24 sts

Row 2 and all even rows: P.

Row 3: [K1, kfb, k1] 8 times. 32 sts

Row 5: [K2, kfb, k1] 8 times. 40 sts

Row 6–14: St st 9 rows.

Row15: [K2, k2tog, k1] 8 times. 32 sts

Row 17: [K1, k2tog, k1] 8 times. 24 sts

Row 19: [K2tog, k1] 8 times. 16 sts

Row 20: [P2tog] 8 times. 8 sts

Row 21: [Kfb] 8 times. 16 sts

Row 23: [K1, kfb] 8 times. 24 sts

Row 25: [K1, kfb, k1] 8 times. 32 sts

Row 26–30: St st 5 rows.

Row 31: [K3, k2tog, k3] 4 times. 28 sts

Row 33: [K2, k2tog, k3] 4 times. 24 sts

Row 35: [K2, k2tog, k2] 4 times. 20 sts

Row 36: P.

Row 37–41: Change to Crepe and g sts 5 rows.

Row 42: Change to Seaspray and p.

Row 43: [K2, k2tog, k1] 4 times. 16 sts

Row 45: [K1, k2tog, k1] 4 times. 12 sts

Row 47: [K1, k2tog] 4 times. 8 sts

Row 48–70: St st 23 rows.

Row 71: [K2tog] 4 times. 4 sts

Break yarn and thread through rem. sts. Pull tight and fasten. Sew along the side edge and stuff. Sew two eyes on the face.

Arms:

Starting from the top of the arm, cast on 6 sts in Latte.

Row 1 and all odd rows: P.

Row 2–3: Cast on 2 st at the beginning of the next 2 rows. 10 sts

Row 4–9: St st 6 rows.

Row 10–11: Change to Crepe and g st 2 rows.

Row 12–14: Change to Latte and st st 3 rows starting with a k row.

Row 15: [P2tog] 5 times. 5 sts

Break yarn and thread through the remaining stitches. Pull tight and fasten. Sew along the edge using mattress stitch up to row 3. Attach to either side of the body.

Turban:

Using Seaspray cast on 48 sts.

Row 1–3: St st 3 rows starting with a p row.

Row 4: P.

Row 5–7: St st 3 rows starting with a p row.

Row 8: [P2, p2tog, p2] 8 times. 40 sts

Row 9: P.

Row 10: K.

Row 11: [P2, p2tog, p1] 8 times. 32 sts

Row 12; P.

Row 13: [P1, p2tog, p1] 8 times. 24 sts

Row 14: K.

Row 15: [P1, p2tog] 8 times. 16 sts

Row 16: P.

Row 17: [P2tog] 8 times. 8 sts

Break yarn and thread through rem. sts. Pull tight and fasten. Wrap around the genie's head, overlapping one side and secure with running sts. Secure the lamp lid to the top of his head.

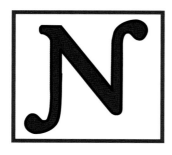

NOBLE STEED

Every true knight needs a noble steed to help him battle ogres and dragons and save damsels in distress. As Shakespeare once wrote: 'A horse, a horse, my kingdom for a horse!'.

YARN USED

- » 100 g (3½ oz) Wendy Merino DK Otter
- » 25 g (¾ oz) Wendy Merino DK Jet
- » 25 g (¾ oz) Wendy Merino DK Crepe
- » 25 g (¾ oz) Wendy Merino DK Persian Red
- » 25 g (¾ oz) Wendy Merino DK Birch

NEEDLES USED

- » 3.5mm (US 4) straight needles

OTHER SUPPLIES

- » Tapestry needle
- » Toy stuffing
- » Crochet hook
- » Two small buttons

INSTRUCTIONS

Body:

With Otter, cast on 16 sts.

Rows 1–2: Work in St st for 2 rows, starting with a k row.

Row 3: K1, [kfb] 14 times, k1. 30 sts

Rows 4–8: Work in St st for 5 rows.

Row 9: K1, [kfb] 28 times, k1. 58 sts

Rows 10–36: Work in St st for 27 rows.

Row 37: K1, [k2tog] 28 times, k1. 30 sts

Rows 38–42: Work in St st for 5 rows.

Row 43: K1, [k2tog] 14 times, k1. 16 sts

Break yarn and draw tail through rem sts, pull tight and fasten. Sew along the back, leaving the neck part open for stuffing.

Neck:

Using Otter cast on 30 sts.

Row 1: K2tog, k26, k2tog. 28 sts

Row 2–4: St st 3 rows.

Row 5: K2tog, k24, k2tog. 26 sts

Row 6–8: St st 3 rows.

Row 9: K2tog, k22, k2tog. 24 sts

Cast off and sew along the side edge. Attach diagonally to the front of the body.

Head:

Using Otter cast on 16 sts.

Row 1: [K1, kfb] 8 times. 24 sts

Row 2 and all even rows: P.

Row 3: [K1, kfb, k1] 8 times. 32 sts

Row 5: [K2, kfb, k1] 8 times. 40 sts

Row 7: K15, change to Birch and k10, change to Otter and k15.

Row 8–16: St st 9 rows, working all Otter sts in otter and all Birch sts in Birch.

Row 17: K16 Otter, k8 Birch, K16 Otter

Row 18: P 17 Otter, P6 Birch, P17 Otter

Row 19–24: St st 6 rows, working all Otter sts in otter and all Birch sts in Birch.

Row 25–32: Change to Birch and st st 8 rows.

Row 33: [K2, k2tog, k1] 8 times. 32 sts

Row 35: [K1, k2tog, k1] 8 times. 24 sts

Row 37: [K1, k2tog] 8 times. 16 sts

Row 38: [P2tog] 8 times. 8 sts

Break yarn and thread through rem. Sts. Pull tight and fasten. Sew along the side edge using mattress sts and stuff. Attach to the neck.

Ears: (make two)

Starting from the bottom of the ears cast on 12 sts in Otter.

Row 1: K1, [kfb] twice, k6, [kfb] twice, k1. 16 sts

Row 2–6: St st 5 rows.

Row 7: [K1, k2tog] twice, k4, [k2tog, k1] twice. 12 sts

Row 8–10: St st 3 rows.

Row 11: K1, [k2tog] twice, k2, [k2tog] twice, k1. 8 sts

Row 12: P.

Row 13: [K2tog] 4 times. 4 sts

Row 14: [P2tog] twice. 2 sts
Cast off. Fold in half and using mattress stitch sew along the side edge. Attach to either side of the head.

Legs: (make four)
Using Otter cast on 20 sts.
Row 1-18: St st 18 rows.
Row 19-25: Change to Birch and st st 6 rows.
Row 26: K.
Row 27: [K1, k2tog, k1] 5 times. 15 sts
Row 28: P.
Row 29: [K1, k2tog] 5 times. 10 sts
Break yarn and thread through rem. Sts. Pull tight and fasten. Using mattress st sew along side edge and stuff. Attach to body.

Blanket:
Refer to chart on the right for detail pattern. Using Crepe cast on 35 sts
Row 1-4: St st 4 rows starting with a k row.
Row 5: K1, *yo, k2tog; rep from * to end.
Row 6-10: St st 5 rows, starting with P row.
Row 11-12: Change to Persian Red and st st 2 rows.
Row 13-19: Repeat the colored pattern.
Row 20-56: Change to Persian Red and st st 37 rows starting with a p row.
Row 57-63: Repeat the colored pattern.
Row 64-65: Change to Persian Red and st st 2 rows, starting with a P row.

Row 66-70: change to Crepe and st st 5 rows, starting with a p row.
Row 71: K1, *yo, k2tog; rep. from * to end.
Row 72-76: St st 5 rows.
Cast off. Fold both cast on edge and cast off edge towards the beginning of the Persian Red rows and secure with running stitches.

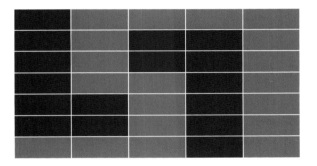

Strap:

Using Persian Red cast on 12 sts.

Row 1: P.

Row 2: K1, yo, k2tog, k6, k2tog, yo, k1.

Row 3: P.

Cast off.

Position the blanket over the horse's back and attach a button on either side below the neck. Button the strap to keep the blanket in place.

Mane:

Cut approximately 50 strands of Jet measuring 20 cm (8 in). Using a crochet hook, create a hair line by inserting the hook at the base of the neck, hooking a strand of jet over and pulling it back. Then insert both ends of the strand through the loop created and pull to fasten. Repeat this in a straight line from the base of the neck to the top of the head, just between the eyes. Create a tail at the back of the body using the same method by hooking strands of yarn in a small circle.

Crochet a chain of 6 sts and then join in the round with a slip stitch. Secure this to the face and the eyes on either side of the head.

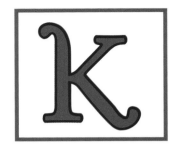

KNIGHT

It used to take years of training to be granted the honorary title of knighthood, often associated with chivalry and a code of honor. Knights spend their days performing heroic acts of bravery and valor across the kingdom, hoping to one-day rescue a princess and becoming her prince charming.

YARN USED

» Wendy Merino DK; 116m (380 ft) per 50 g (2 oz) ball; 100% Merino wool
» 50 g (2 oz) Wendy Merino DK Smoke
» 50 g (2 oz) Wendy Merino DK Blue Lagoon
» 50 g (2 oz) Wendy Merino DK Wind Chime
» 25 g (2 oz) Wendy Merino DK Phlox
» 25 g (¾ oz) Wendy Merino DK Mulberry
» 25 g (¾ oz) Wendy Merino DK Crepe
» 25 g (¾ oz) Wendy Merino DK Persian Red
» Scrap amounts of white and pink for the mouth and eyes.

NEEDLES USED

» 3.5mm (US 4) straight needles
» 2, 3.5mm (US 4) double pointed needles

OTHER SUPPLIES

» Tapestry needle
» Stuffing
» Crochet hook
» 2 small buttons
» Scissors

INSTRUCTIONS

Legs: (make two)

Starting from the bottom of the foot cast on 22 sts using Smoke.

Row 1 and all odd rows: Purl.

Row 2: K1, [kfb] 20 times, k1. 42 sts

Rows 3–17: Work in St st for 15 rows.

Row 18: K7, [k2tog] 14 times, k7. 28 sts

Row 20: K7, [k2tog] 7 times, k7. 21 sts

Rows 21–63: Change to Blue Lagoon and st st for 43 rows.

Row 64: K4, [k2tog] twice, k5, [k2tog] twice, k4. 17 sts

Cast off loosely. Sew up the bottom of the foot first and continue along the back edge, leaving the cast off edge open. Stuff and knit a second identical leg.

Boot cuffs: (make two)

Using Smoke cast on 24 sts.

Row 1–2: St st 2 rows starting with a k row.

Row 3: [K2, kfb,k3] 4 times. 28 sts

Row 4–8: St st 5 rows.

Row 9: [K3, kfb,k3] 4 times. 32 sts

Row 10–14: St st 5 rows.

Cast off and position around the leg. Join the side seam and secure to the top of the shoe.

Body and head:

Starting at the bottom, cast on 14 sts using Blue Lagoon.

Rows 1–2: Work in St st for 2 rows.

Row 3: [Kfb] 14 times. 28 sts

Row 5: [Kfb] 28 times. 56 sts

Rows 6–30: Work in St st for 25 rows.

Row 31: Change to Wind Chime and [k2tog] 28 times. 28 sts

Rows 32–36: Work in St st for 5 rows.

Row 37: [K2tog] 14 times. 14 sts

Row 38 and all even rows: P.

Row 39: [Kfb] 14 times. 28 sts

Row 41: [K1, kfb] 14 times. 42 sts

Row 43: [K1, kfb, k1] 14 times. 56 sts

Row 45: [K2, kfb, k1] 14 times. 70 sts

Row 46–64: St st 19 sts.

Row 65: [K2, k2tog, k1] 14 times. 56 sts

Row 67: [K1, k2tog, k1] 14 times. 42 sts

Row 69: [K1, k2tog] 14 times. 28 sts

Row 71: [K2tog] 14 times. 14 sts

Row 72: [P2tog] 7 times. 7 sts

Break yarn and draw through rem sts, pull tight and fasten. Sew along the back using mattress st and stuff.

For the eyes, use a crochet hook to create a chain of 6 sts in white or beige and join in the round with a loop stitch. Secure to either side of the face. Using your preferred eye color sew the pupils in place. Add a nose in face color and eyebrows in hair color. Sew a mouth using back stitch. Close the cast on edge of the body. Sew both legs to the bottom.

Arm – Right hand:

Starting from the fingers, cast on 6 sts in Smoke on a dpn.

Row 1–4: Work an i-cord for 4 rows.

Row 5: Cast off 3 sts, k to end. Leave the remaining sts waiting. Make 3 more fingers and place all 4 fingers together with the wrong side facing.

Row 6: Cast on 12 sts, p across the 4 fingers. 24 sts.

Row 7: [K2, k2tog, k2] 4 times. 20 sts

Row 8 and all even rows: P. Leave these 20 sts waiting and make a 5th i-cord of 6 sts.

Row 1–4: Work the i-cord for 4 rows.

Row 9: K across the icord, then join and k the 20 waiting sts. 26 sts

Row 11: K1, [k2, k2tog, k2] 4 times, k1. 22 sts

Row 13: K1, [k2, k2tog, k1] 4 times, k1. 18 sts

Row 14–39: Change to Blue Lagoon and st st 26 rows.

Row 40: Cast off 9 sts, p to end. 9 sts

Row 41: K2tog, k5, k2tog. 7 sts

Row 43: K2tog, k3, k2tog. 5 sts

Row 45: K2tog, k1, k2tog. 3 sts

Cast off and sew the bottom of the fingers to the palm on the hand and along the side edge. Stuff and attach to either side of the body.

Arm – Left hand:

Make 4 i-cords as for the right hand but place them on the straight needles with the right side facing and work as followed:

Row 6: P across all for fingers (12 sts), cast on 12 sts. 24 sts

Row 7: [K2, k2tog, k2] 4 times. 20 sts

Row 8 and all even rows: P. Leave these 20 sts waiting and make a 5th i-cord of 6 sts.

Row 1–4: Work the i-cord for 4 rows.

Row 9: Join yarn to the 20 sts waiting. K20 and then knit across the 6 icord sts. 26 sts.

Row 10: P.

Row 11: K1, [k2, k2tog, k2] 4 times, k1. 22 sts

Row 13: K1, [k2, k2tog, k1] 4 times, k1. 18 sts

Row 14–40: Change to Blue Lagoon and st st 27 rows.

Row 41: Cast off 10 sts, k to the last 2 sts, k2tog. 7 sts

Row 43: K2tog, k3, k2tog. 5 sts

Row 45: K2tog, k1, k2tog. 3 sts

Cast off and sew as you did the right hand.

Gauntlets: (make two)

Using Smoke cast on 20 sts.

Row 1: P.

Row 2: [K2, kfb, k2] 4 times. 24 sts

Row 3: P.

Row 5: [K3, kfb, k2] 4 times. 28 sts
Cast off. Position around the wrist and join the side edge with mattress st. Secure to the wrist with running sts.

Hairpiece:
Using Crepe cast on 72 sts.
Row 1–10: St st 10 rows.
Row 11: [K3, k2tog, k3] 9 times. 63 sts
Row 12 and all even rows: P.
Row 13: [K2, k2tog, k3] 9 times. 54 sts
Row 15: [K2, k2tog, k2] 9 times. 45 sts
Row 17: [K1, k2tog, k2] 9 times. 36 sts
Row 19: [K1, k2tog, k1] 9 times. 27 sts
Row 21: [K2tog, k1] 9 times. 18 sts
Row 22: [P2tog] 9 times. 9 sts
Break yarn and thread through rem sts. Pull tight and fasten. Using mattress stitch sew along the side edge and position diagonal on the head. Attach with a running stitch. For the hair, cut approximately 50 strands of Crepe measuring about 10 cm (4 in) in length. Fold a strand of hair in half, insert the crochet hook into the edge of the hair cap, hook the middle of the strand over the hook, pull back and then insert both ends of the strand through the loop created. Pull tight to secure. Continue to do this all along the edge of the hair cap and then again in smaller circles towards the center of the head. Trim as desired.

Tabard:
Cast on 15 sts in Mulberry and 15 sts in Persian Red using a cable cast on. When starting your first row you should have 15 Persian Red sts first, followed by 15 Mulberry sts.
Row 1–24: St st 24 rows, working the colors as they present themselves on the needle.
Row 25: K15 in Mulberry and 15 in Persian Red.
Row 26–48: St st 23 rows, working the colors as they present themselves on the needle.
Row 49: Change to Persian Red and k8, cast off 7 sts, change to Mulberry cast off 7 sts, k to end. 16 sts
Row 50: Using Mulberry, p8, cast on 7 sts, change to red and cast on 7 sts, p to end. 30 sts
Row 51–74: St st 24 rows, working the colors as they present themselves on the needle.
Row 75: K15 in Mulberry and k15 in Persian Red.
Row 76–98: St st 23 rows, working the colors as they present themselves on the needle.
Cast off in respective colors. Put the vest on the knight's body and secure the side seams with mattress sts.

Cape:

Using Phlox cast on 40 sts.

Row 1–56: St st 56 rows starting with a
k row.

Row 57: [K2tog] 10 times, turn and leave
the rem. 20 sts waiting. 10 sts

Row 58 and all even rows: P.

Row 59: [K2tog] 5 times. 5 sts

Row 61: K1, k2tog, yo, k2.

Row 62: P.

Cast off and join yarn to the rem. 20 sts
waiting and repeat rows 57–62.

Attach a button to either side of the
shoulder part of the vest, positioned to
match up with the button holes on the cape.

Emblem:

Using Crepe cast on 12 sts

Row 1–2: G sts 2 rows.

Row 3 (RS): K3, change to Phlox and k6,
carrying color changes to the back, k3 in
Crepe.

Row 4: K3 in crepe, p6 in Phlox, k3 in Crepe.

Row 5–8: Repeat rows 3 and 4 twice.

Row 9: K3 in Crepe, Change to Phlox and
k2tog, k2, k2tog, then k3 in Crepe. 10 sts

Row 10: K3 in crepe, [p2tog] twice in Phlox,
k3 in Crepe. 8 sts

From here on continue working in Crepe
only.

Row 11: [K2tog] 4 times. 4 sts

Row 12: K.

Row 13: [K2tog] twice. 2 sts

Cast off. Sew the emblem to the front
of the knight's vest. If desired you could
embroider a symbol on the crest, such as
a cross, sword, lightening, flower, star,
diamond, heart, leaf, letter, number,
emoticon, etc.

MERLIN

Merlin was a powerful and wise wizard who appeared in many fairy tales, usually giving council to a king or prince in need of advice. He would not simply perform magic but also school his visitors with his infinite wisdom about the world.

YARN USED

» Wendy Merino DK; 116m (380 ft) per 50 g (2 oz) ball; 100% Merino wool
» 50 g (2 oz) Wendy Merino DK Periwinkle
» 50 g (2 oz) Wendy Merino DK Wind Chime
» 25 g (¾ oz) Wendy Merino DK Jet
» 25 g (¾ oz) Wendy Merino DK Silver
» A small amount of Crepe

NEEDLES USED

» 3.5mm (US 4) straight needles

OTHER SUPPLIES

» Tapestry needle
» Stuffing

INSTRUCTIONS

Legs: (make two)

Starting from the bottom of the foot cast on 19 sts using Jet.

Row 1 and all odd rows: Purl.

Row 2: K1, [kfb] 16 times, k2. 35 sts

Rows 3–11: Work in St st for 9 rows.

Row 12: K4, [k2tog] 13 times, k5. 22 sts

Row 14: K3, [k2tog] 8 times, k3. 14 sts

Rows 15–35: Change to Wind Chime and work st st for 21 rows starting with a p row.

Row 36: K2, [k2tog] twice, k2, [k2tog] twice, k2. 10 sts

Cast off loosely. Sew up the bottom of the foot first and continue along the back edge, leaving the cast off edge open. Stuff and knit a second identical leg.

Body and head:

Starting at the bottom, cast on 14 sts using Wind Chime.

Rows 1–2: Work in St st for 2 rows.

Row 3: K1, [kfb] 12 times, k1. 26 sts

Row 4 and all even rows: P.

Row 5: K1, [k1, kfb] 12 times, k1. 38 sts

Rows 6–20: Work in St st for 15 rows.

Row 21: K1, [k1, k2tog] 12 times, k1. 26 sts

Rows 22–26: Work in St st for 5 rows.

Row 27: K1, [k2tog] 12 times, k1. 14 sts

Row 29: [Kfb] 14 times. 28 sts

Row 31: [K1, kfb] 14 times. 42 sts

Row 33: [K1, kfb, k1] 14 times. 56 sts

Row 34–52: St st 19 sts.

Row 53: [K1, k2tog, k1] 14 times. 42 sts

Row 55: [K1, k2tog] 14 times. 28 sts

Row 57: [K2tog] 14 times. 14 sts

Row 58: [P2tog] 7 times. 7 sts

Break yarn and draw through rem sts, pull tight and fasten. Using mattress sts sew along the side edge and stuff before closing. Attach the legs to the body.

Arms: (make two)

Using Wind Chime cast on 8 sts.

Row 1: K.

Row 2: Cast on 2 sts, p to end. 10 sts

Row 3: Cast on 2 sts, k to end. 12 sts

Row 4–26: St st 23 rows, starting with a k row.

Row 27: [K2tog] 6 times. 6 sts

Break yarn and thread through rem. Sts. Pull tight and fasten. Using mattress stitch sew along the side edge and attach to either side of the body.

Robe:

Using Periwinkle cast on 80 sts.

Row 1–6: St st 6 rows starting with a k row.

Row 7: [K4, k2tog, k4] 8 times. 72 sts

Row 8–12: St st 5 rows.

Row 13: [K3, k2tog, k4] 8 times. 64 sts

Row 14–18: St st 5 rows.

Row 19: [K2, k2tog, k4] 8 times. 56 sts

Row 20-24: St st 5 rows.

Row 25: [K1, k2tog, k4] 8 times. 48 sts

Row 26-30: St st 5 rows.

Row 31: [K2tog, k4] 8 times. 40 sts

Row 32-36: St st 5 rows.

Row 37: K8, cast off 5 sts, k14, cast off 5 sts, k8. 30 sts

Continue working on the first 8 sts, leaving the other sts waiting.

Row 38-39: St st 2 rows.

Row 40: Cast off 4 sts, p to end. 4 sts

Row 41-42: St st 2 rows.

Cast off. Join yarn to the middle 14 sts.

Row 38-39: St st 2 rows.

Row 40: P4, cast off 6 sts, p4. 8 sts

Row 41-42: St st 2 rows in the first 4 sts, then cast off. Repeat for the next 4 sts waiting.

Join yarn to the rem. 8 sts.

Row 38: P.

Row 39: Cast off 4 sts, k to end 4 sts

Row 40-42: St st 3 rows. Cast off.

Using mattress sts join both shoulder parts together and seam up the back of the dress, starting from the bottom up to the last 5 rows. This small opening at the back will make it easier to dress Merlin. If desired you could attach a small button to one side and create a chain of crochet sts on the other to secure or simply sew it all up once he has been dressed.

Sleeves: (Make two)

Using Periwinkle cast on 6 sts

Row 1: [Kfb] twice, k2, [kfb] twice. 10 sts

Row 2 and all even rows: P.

Row 3: [Kfb] twice, k6, [kfb] twice. 14 sts

Row 5: [Kfb] twice, k10, [kfb] twice. 18 sts

Row 6-8: St st 3 rows.

Row 9: [Kfb] twice, k14, [kfb] twice. 22 sts

Row 10-12: St st 3 rows.

Row 13: [Kfb] twice, k18, [kfb] twice. 26 sts

Row 14-16: St st 3 rows.

Row 17: [Kfb] twice, k22, [kfb] twice. 30 sts

Row 18-20: St st 3 rows.

Row 21: [Kfb] twice. K26, [kfb] twice. 34 sts

Row 22-24: St st 3 rows.

Cast off and sew along the side edge up to row 6 using mattress stitches, then secure in the sleeve opening of the robe.

Hat:

Using Periwinkle cast on 56 sts.

Row 1-8: St st 8 rows, starting with a k row.

Row 9: [K3, k2tog, k3] 7 times. 49 sts

Row 10-12: St st 3 rows.

Row 13: [K3, k2tog, k2] 7 times. 42 sts

Row 14-16: St st 3 rows.

Row 17: [K2, k2tog, k2] 7 times. 35 sts

Row 18-20: St st 3 rows.

Row 21: [K2, k2tog, k1] 7 times. 28 sts

Row 22-24: St st 3 rows.

Row 25: [K1, k2tog, k1] 7 times. 21 sts

Row 26-28: St st 3 rows.

Row 29: [K1, k2tog] 7 times. 14 sts
Row 30 and all even rows: P.
Row 31: [K2tog] 7 times. 7 sts
Break yarn and thread through rem. Sts.
Pull tight and fasten. Using mattress st sew
along the side edge.

Embroider lazy daisies (see opposite for
photo tutorial) all over the front and back of
the robe and on the hat using Crepe.

Cut approximately 70 strands of Silver
measuring about 15 cm (6 in). Insert the
crochet hook through the back of a stitch
on the inside of the hat and pull a strand
halfway through. Next insert the two ends
of the strand through the loop created and
pull tight. Repeat this all around the hat,
then stuff and secure to the head. Using
Periwinkle sew two eyes in place and
repeat the same technique for the hair to
create a moustache by hooking 8 strands
under the eyes and then a beard by hooking
approximately 16 strands in a line curving
upwards like a smile underneath the
moustache.

LAZY DAISIES TUTORIAL

Starting from the center of the flower,
create a loop.

Insert your needle into the center of the
flower and exit through the inner part of the
first petal.

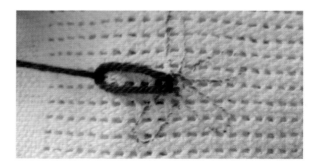

Insert your needle just outside the first petal and exit through the center of the flower. This creates the first petal.

Repeat for the remaining 4 petals, finishing in the center.

MERMAID

Mermaids are legendary aquatic creatures with the head and torso of a human and the tail of a fish. They get to roam the depths of the sea and live in amazing underwater palaces. Sadly, they often fall in love with humans, leaving them wanting to trade their tail fin for a pair of legs so they can be with their true love.

YARN USED

- » Wendy Merino DK; 116m (380 ft) per 50g ball; 100% Merino wool
- » 50 g (2 oz) Wendy Merino DK Phlox
- » 50 g (2 oz) Wendy Merino DK Wind Chime
- » 50 g (2 oz) Wendy Merino DK Fennel
- » 50 g (2 oz) Wendy Merino DK Carnation
- » 25 g (¾ oz) Wendy Merino DK Cloud Dancer

NEEDLES USED

- » 3.5mm (US 4) straight needles

OTHER SUPPLIES

- » Tapestry needle
- » Stuffing
- » Crochet hook

INSTRUCTIONS

Legs: (make two)

Starting from the bottom of the foot cast on 16 sts using Phlox.

Row 1 and all odd rows: Purl.

Row 2: K1, [kfb] 14 times, k1. 30 sts

Rows 3–11: Work in St st for 9 rows.

Row 12: K5, [k2tog] 10 times, k5. 20 sts

Row 14: K5, [k2tog] 5 times, k5. 15 sts

Rows 15–21: Change to Cloud Dancer and st st 7 rows.

Row 22: P.

Row 23–51: Change to Wind Chime and work st st for 29 rows starting with a P row.

Row 52: K2, [k2tog] twice, k3, [k2tog] twice, k2. 11 sts

Cast off loosely. Sew up the bottom of the foot first and continue along the back edge, leaving the cast off edge open. Stuff and knit a second identical leg.

Body and head:

Starting at the bottom, cast on 12 sts using Wind Chime.

Rows 1–2: Work in St st for 2 rows.

Row 3: [Kfb] 12 times. 24 sts

Row 5: [K1, kfb] 12 times. 36 sts

Rows 6–30: Work in St st for 25 rows.

Row 31: [K1, k2tog] 12 times. 24 sts

Rows 32–36: Work in St st for 5 rows.

Row 37: [K2tog] 12 times. 12 sts

Row 38 and all even rows: P.

Row 39: [Kfb] 12 times. 24 sts

Row 41: [K1, kfb] 12 times. 36 sts

Row 43: [K1, kfb, k1] 12 times. 48 sts

Row 45: [K2, kfb, k1] 12 times. 60 sts

Row 46–64: St st 19 sts.

Row 65: [K2, k2tog, k1] 12 times. 48 sts

Row 67: [K1, k2tog, k1] 12 times. 36 sts

Row 69: [K1, k2tog] 12 times. 24 sts

Row 71: [K2tog] 12 times. 12 sts

Row 72: [P2tog] 6 times. 6 sts

Break yarn and draw through rem sts, pull tight and fasten. Using mattress sts sew along the side edge and stuff before closing. Attach the legs to the body.

Arms: (make two)

Using Wind Chime cast on 8 sts.

Row 1: K.

Row 2: Cast on 2 sts, p to end. 10 sts

Row 3: Cast on 2 sts, k to end. 12 sts

Row 4–34: St st 31 rows, starting with a p row.

Row 35: [K2tog] 6 times. 6 sts

Break yarn and thread through rem. Sts. Pull tight and fasten. Using mattress stitch sew along the side edge and attach to either side of the body.

Hair cap:

Using Fennel cast on 64 sts.

Row 1–8: St st 8 rows starting with a k row.

Row 9: [K3, k2tog, k3] 8 times. 56 sts

Row 10 and all even rows: P.

Row 11: [K3, k2tog, k2] 8 times. 48 sts

Row 13: [K2, k2tog, k2] 8 times. 40 sts

Row 15: [K2, k2tog, k1] 8 times. 32 sts

Row 17: [K1, k2tog, k1] 8 times. 24 sts

Row 19: [K1, k2tog] 8 times. 16 sts

Row 20: [P2tog] 8 times. 8 sts

Break yarn and thread through rem. Sts.
Pull tight and fasten. Position diagonally on
the Mermaid's head, joining side edges at
back of head and secure with running sts.

Hair:

Wrap Fennel and Carnation yarn around
a dvd case and cut along one side. Place
two strands of Fennel and one strand of
Carnation in the middle of the scalp and
secure using a backstitch. Repeat along the
length of the head. Next using whip stitches
sew a fringe in Fennel below the hairline,
starting each strand from the same point.

Mermaid outfit:

Using Carnation cast on 40 sts.

Row 1 and 2: *K2, p2; rep. from * to end.

Row 3 and 4: *P2, k2; rep. from * to end.

Row 5–12: Repeat rows 1–4.

Row 13: Change to Fennel and [Kfb] 40

times. 80 sts

Row 14: (Wrong Side): P3, *k2, p4,* rep
from * to last 3 sts, p3.

Row 15: K3, *sl 2, k4,* rep from * to last
3 sts, k3.

Row 16: P3, *sl 2, p4,* rep from * to last
3 sts, p3.

Row 17: K1, *sl next 2 sts on spare needle
and leave at back, k1, k 2 off the spare
needle, sl next stitch on spare needle,
and leave at front, k2, k1 off spare
needle,* repeat from * to last stitch, k1.

Row 18: P6, *k2, p4,* rep from * to last
6 sts, p6.

Row 19: K6, *sl 2, k4,* rep from * to last
6 sts, k6.

Row 20: P6, *sl 2, p4,* rep from * to last
6 sts, p6.

Row 21: K4, *sl next 2 sts on spare needle
and leave at back, k1, k 2 off spare
needle, sl next stitch on spare needle and
leave at front, k2, k 1 off spare needle,*
repeat from * to last 4 sts, k4.

Row 22–37: Repeat rows 14–21.

Row 38: P3, *k2, p4,* rep from * to last
3 sts, p3.

Row 39: K3, *sl 2, k4,* rep from * to last
3 sts, k3.

Row 40: P3, *sl 2, p4,* rep from * to last
3 sts, p3.

Row 41: K1, *sl next 2 sts on spare needle
and leave at back, k1, k 2 off the spare

needle, sl next stitch on spare needle, and leave at front, k2, k1 off spare needle,* repeat from * to last stitch, k1.

Row 42: [P2tog] 3 times, *k2, p4,* rep from * to last 6 sts, [p2tog] 3 times. 74 sts

Row 43: K3, *sl 2, k4,* rep from * to last 3 sts, k3.

Row 44: P3, *sl 2, p4,* rep from * to last 3 sts, p3.

Row 45: K1, *sl next 2 sts on spare needle and leave at back, k1, k 2 off the spare needle, sl next stitch on spare needle, and leave at front, k2, k1 off spare needle,* repeat from * to last stitch, k1.

Row 46: [P2tog] 3 times, *k2, p4,* rep from * to last 6 sts, [p2tog] 3 times. 68 sts

Row 47: K3, *sl 2, k4,* rep from * to last 3 sts, k3.

Row 48: P3, *sl 2, p4,* rep from * to last 3 sts, p3.

Row 49: K1, *sl next 2 sts on spare needle and leave at back, k1, k 2 off the spare needle, sl next stitch on spare needle, and leave at front, k2, k1 off spare needle,* repeat from * to last stitch, k1.

Row 50: [P2tog] 3 times, *k2, p4,* rep from * to last 6 sts, [p2tog] 3 times. 62 sts

Row 51: K3, *sl 2, k4,* rep from * to last 3 sts, k3.

Row 52: P3, *sl 2, p4,* rep from * to last 3 sts, p3.

Row 53: K1, *sl next 2 sts on spare needle

and leave at back, k1, k2 off the spare needle, sl next stitch on spare needle, and leave at front, k2, k1 off spare needle,* repeat from * to last stitch, k1.

Row 54: [P2tog] 3 times, *k2, p4,* rep from * to last 6 sts, [p2tog] 3 times. 56 sts

Row 55: K3, *sl 2, k4,* rep from * to last 3 sts, k3.

Row 56: P3, *sl 2, p4,* rep from * to last 3 sts, p3.

Row 57: K1, *sl next 2 sts on spare needle and leave at back, k1, k 2 off the spare needle, sl next stitch on spare needle, and leave at front, k2, k1 off spare needle,* repeat from * to last stitch, k1.

Row 58: [P2tog] 3 times, *k2, p4,* rep from * to last 6 sts, [p2tog] 3 times. 50 sts

Row 59: K3, *sl 2, k4,* rep from * to last 3 sts, k3.

Row 60: P3, *sl 2, p4,* rep from * to last 3 sts, p3.

Row 61: K1, *sl next 2 sts on spare needle and leave at back, k1, k 2 off the spare needle, sl next stitch on spare needle, and leave at front, k2, k1 off spare needle,* repeat from * to last stitch, k1.

Row 62: [P2tog] 3 times, *k2, p4,* rep from * to last 6 sts, [p2tog] 3 times. 44 sts

Row 63: K3, *sl 2, k4,* rep from * to last 3 sts, k3.

Row 64: P3, *sl 2, p4,* rep from * to last 3 sts, p3.

Row 65: K1, *sl next 2 sts on spare needle and leave at back, k1, k 2 off the spare needle, sl next stitch on spare needle, and leave at front, k2, k1 off spare needle,* repeat from * to last stitch, k1.

Row 66: [P2tog] 3 times, *k2, p4,* rep from * to last 6 sts, [p2tog] 3 times. 38 sts

Row 67: K3, *sl 2, k4,* rep from * to last 3 sts, k3.

Row 68: P3, *sl 2, p4,* rep from * to last 3 sts, p3.

Row 69: K1, *sl next 2 sts on spare needle and leave at back, k1, k 2 off the spare needle, sl next stitch on spare needle, and leave at front, k2, k1 off spare needle,* repeat from * to last stitch, k1.

Row 70: [P2tog] 3 times, *k2, p4,* rep from * to last 6 sts, [p2tog] 3 times. 32 sts

Row 71: K3, *sl 2, k4,* rep from * to last 3 sts, k3.

Row 72: P3, *sl 2, p4,* rep from * to last 3 sts, p3.

Row 73: K1, *sl next 2 sts on spare needle and leave at back, k1, k 2 off the spare needle, sl next stitch on spare needle, and leave at front, k2, k1 off spare needle,* repeat from * to last stitch, k1.

Row 74: P16 and turn, leaving the rem. 16 sts waiting. 16 sts

Row 75: K1, [kfb] twice, k2, [kfb] twice, k2, [kfb] twice, k2, [kfb] twice, k1. 24 sts

Row 76 and all even rows: P.

Row 77: K1, [kfb] twice, k6, [kfb] twice, k2, [kfb] twice, k6, [kfb] twice, k1. 32 sts

Row 78–80: St st 3 rows.

Row 81: [K1, k2tog, k10, k2tog, k1] twice. 28 sts

Row 83: [K1, k2tog, k8, k2tog, k1] twice. 24 sts

Row 85: [K1, k2tog, k6, k2tog, k1] twice. 20 sts

Row 86–88: St st 3 rows.

Row 89: [K1, k2tog, k4, k2tog, k1] twice. 16 sts

Row 90–92: St st 3 rows.

Row 93: [K1, k2tog, k2, k2tog, k1] twice. 12 sts

Row 94–96: St st 3 rows.

Row 97: [K1, k2tog, k2tog, k1] twice. 8 sts

Row 98–100: St st 3 rows.

Row 101: [K2tog] 4 times. 4 sts

Row 102: [P2tog] twice. 2 sts

Break yarn and thread through rem. Sts. Pull tight and fasten. Pick up the rem. 16 sts and repeat rows 74–94. Sew along the side edge using mattress stitches.

Straps:

Using Carnation cast on 16 sts.

Row 1–4: St st 4 rows.

Attach the straps vertically to the outfit and secure at the back using mattress sts.

Dress:

Using Carnation cast on 80 sts.

Row 1: K.

Row 2: Change to Phlox and k1, sl1, *k4, sl2; rep from * to the last 6 sts, k4, sl1, k1.

Row 3: P1, sl1, *p4, sl2; rep. from * to last 6 sts, p4, sl1, p1.

Row 4: Change to Carnation and repeat row 2.

Row 5: K1, sl1 wyif, *k4, sl2 wyif,; rep from * to last 6 sts, k4, sl1 wyif, k1.

Row 6: Change to Phlox and k3, *sl2, k4; rep from * to last 5 sts, sl2, k3.

Row 7: P3, *sl2, p4; rep. from * to last 5 sts, sl2, p3.

Row 8: Change to carnation and k3, *sl2, k4; rep from * to last 5 sts, sl2, k3.

Row 9: K3, *sl2 wyif, k4; rep. from * to last 5 sts, sl2 wyif, k3.

Row 10–81: Repeat rows 2–9.

Row 82: Change to Plox and [k2tog] 40 times. 40 sts

Row 83–95: St st 13 rows.

Row 96: Change to 2365 and k8, cast off 5 sts, k14, cast off 5 sts, k8. 30 sts

Row 97: K8, cast on 10 sts, k14, cast on 10 sts, k8. 50 sts

Row 98–101: G st 4 rows.

Cast off and sew along the side edge.

OGRE

Every good fairy tale needs an ogre... but all this little guy wants is a hug! His long dangly arms are perfect for wrapping around your shoulders so you can give this little ogre a nice big squeeze!

YARN USED

» Wendy Merino DK; 116m (380 ft) per 50g (2 oz) ball; 100% Merino wool
» 100 g (3½ oz) Wendy merino DK Mulberry
» 50 g (2 oz) Wendy Merino DK Persian Red
» 50 g (2 oz) Wendy Merino DK Seaspray
» A scrap amount of Birch (beige)

NEEDLES USED

» 3.5mm (US 4) straight needles

OTHER SUPPLIES

» Tapestry needle
» Stuffing
» Two small black buttons
» Two big white buttons

INSTRUCTIONS

Body:

Using Mulberry cast on 8 sts.

Row 1: [Kfb] 8 times. 16 sts

Row 2 and all even rows: P.

Row 3: [k1, kfb] 8 times. 24 sts

Row 5: [K1, kfb, k1] 8 times. 32 sts

Row 7: [K2, kfb, k1] 8 times. 40 sts

Row 9: [K2, kfb, k2] 8 times. 48 sts

Row 11: [K3, kfb, k2] 8 times. 56 sts

Row 13: [K3, kfb, k3] 8 times. 64 sts

Row 15: [K4, kfb, k3] 8 times. 72 sts.

Row 17: [K4, kfb, k4] 8 times. 80 sts

Row 18–60: St st 43 rows.

Row 61: [K1, k2tog, k1] 20 times. 60 sts

Row 63: [K1, kfb] 30 times. 90 sts

Row 64–76: St st 13 rows.

Row 77: Leave the first 22 sts waiting, k46, leave the other 22 sts waiting. 46 sts

Row 78–90: St st 13 rows on the middle 46 sts only. Then cast off the 46 sts.

Row 91: Pick up and k the first 22 sts, cast on and k 46 sts, pick up and k the last 22 sts. 90 sts

Row 92–96: St st 5 rows.

Row 97: K1, [k5, k2tog, k4] 8 times, k1. 82 sts

Row 99: K1, [k4, k2tog, k4] 8 times, k1. 74 sts

Row 101: K1, [k4, k2tog, k3] 8 times, k1. 66 sts

Row 103: K1, [k3, k2tog, k3] 8 times, k1. 58 sts

Row 105: K1, [k3, k2tog, k2] 8 times, k1. 50 sts

Row 107: K1, [k2, k2tog, k2] 8 times, k1. 42 sts

Row 109: K1, [k2, k2tog, k1] 8 times, k1. 34 sts

Row 111: K1, [k1, k2tog, k1] 8 times, k1. 26 sts

Row 113: K1, [k1, k2tog] 8 times, k1. 18 sts

Row 114: [P2tog] 9 times. 9 sts

Break yarn and thread through rem. sts. Pull tight and fasten. Using mattress st sew along the side edge and stuff. Close the cast on edge. Fold the 46 middle sts inwards and stuff to create a lip. Using running sts secure the cast off edge of the lip to the inside of the face, just above the increase row (row 63). Attach the top of the lip to the front of the face. Using tweezers insert some stuffing to bulge out the lip. Attach two white buttons for eyes and two black buttons for pupils.

Tooth:

Using Birch cast on 9 sts.

Row 1–3: St st 3 rows starting with a p row.

Row 4: K2tog, k5, k2tog. 7 sts

Row 5 and all odd rows: P.

Row 6: K2tog, k3, k2tog. 5 sts

Row 8: K2tog, k1, k2tog. 3 sts

Break yarn and thread through rem. sts.

Pull tight and fasten. Sew along the side edge and attach behind the lip.

Arms:

Using Mulberry cast on 16 sts.

Row 1–60: St st 60 rows starting with a k row.

Row 61: [K1, kfb] 8 times. 24 sts

Row 62 and all even rows: P.

Row 63: [K1, kfb, k1] 8 times. 32 sts

Row 65: [k2, kfb, k1] 8 times. 40 sts

Row 66–76: St st 11 rows.

Row 77: [K2, k2tog, k1] 8 times. 32 sts

Row 79: [K1, k2tog, k1] 8 times. 24 sts

Row 81: [K1, k2tog] 8 times. 16 sts

Row 83: [K2tog] 8 times. 8 sts

Break yarn and thread through rem. sts. Pull tight and fasten. Using mattress stitch sew along the side edge and stuff the hand only. Secure to either side of the body.

Legs:

Using Persian Red cast on 16 sts

Row 1–64: St st 64 rows starting with a k row, alternating Persian red and Seaspray after every 4 rows.

Row 65: Change to Persian Red and [k1, kfb] 8 times. 24 sts

Row 66 and all even rows: P.

Row 67: [K1, kfb, k1] 8 times. 32 sts

Row 69: [k2, kfb, k1] 8 times. 40 sts

Row 70–80: St st 11 rows.

Row 81: [K2, k2tog, k1] 8 times. 32 sts

Row 83: [K1, k2tog, k1] 8 times. 24 sts

Row 85: [K1, k2tog] 8 times. 16 sts

Row 87: [K2tog] 8 times. 8 sts

Break yarn and thread through rem. sts. Pull tight and fasten. Using mattress stitch sew along the side edge and stuff the hand only. Secure to either side of the body.

PRINCESS

Princesses are often in the middle of all sorts of peril in fairy tales and often need rescuing from dragons, ogres, witches or tall towers. They can always rely on other fairy tale creatures to come to their aide and save the day.

YARN USED

» Wendy Merino DK; 116m (380 ft) per 50 g (2 oz) ball; 100% Merino wool
» 50 g (2 oz) Wendy Merino DK Wind Chime
» 50 g (2 oz) Wendy Merino DK Watermelon
» 50 g (2 oz) Wendy Merino DK Mulberry
» 25 g (¾ oz) Wendy Merino DK Crepe
» 25 g (¾ oz) Wendy Merino DK Otter
» A small amount of black and blue for the eyes.

NEEDLES USED

» 3.5mm (US 4) straight needles
» 3.5 mm (US 4) double pointed needles

OTHER SUPPLIES

» Tapestry needle
» Stuffing
» Scissors
» Crochet hook

INSTRUCTIONS

Legs: (make two)

Starting from the bottom of the foot cast on 22 sts using Watermelon.

Row 1 and all odd rows: Purl.

Row 2: K1, [kfb] 20 times, k1. 42 sts

Rows 3–17: Work in St st for 15 rows.

Row 18: K7, [k2tog] 14 times, k7. 28 sts

Row 20: K7, [k2tog] 7 times, k7. 21 sts

Rows 21–63: Change to Wind Chime and st st for 43 rows.

Row 64: K4, [k2tog] twice, k5, [k2tog] twice, k4. 17 sts

Cast off loosely. Sew up the bottom of the foot first and continue along the back edge, leaving the cast off edge open. Stuff and knit a second identical leg.

Body:

Starting at the bottom, cast on 14 sts using Watermelon.

Rows 1–2: Work in St st for 2 rows.

Row 3: [Kfb] 14 times. 28 sts

Row 5: [Kfb] 28 times. 56 sts

Rows 6–24: Work in St st for 19 rows.

Row 25–30: Change to Wind Chime and st st 6 rows.

Row 31: [K2tog] 28 times. 28 sts

Rows 32–36: Work in St st for 5 rows.

Row 37: [K2tog] 14 times. 14 sts

Row 38 and all even rows: P.

Row 39: [Kfb] 14 times. 28 sts

Row 41: [K1, kfb] 14 times. 42 sts

Row 43: [K1, kfb, k1] 14 times. 56 sts

Row 45: [K2, kfb, k1] 14 times. 70 sts

Row 46–64: St st 19 sts.

Row 65: [K2, k2tog, k1] 14 times. 56 sts

Row 67: [K1, k2tog, k1] 14 times. 42 sts

Row 69: [K1, k2tog] 14 times. 28 sts

Row 71: [K2tog] 14 times. 14 sts

Row 72: [P2tog] 7 times. 7 sts

Break yarn and draw through rem sts, pull tight and fasten. Sew along the back using mattress sts and stuff. Attach the legs to the bottom of the body.

For the eyes, create a chain of 6 sts in beige and join in the round with a slip stitch. Secure to the face. Backstitch a line of black around the eye and add two small streaks for eye lashes. Using blue whip stitch the pupils and add some black and white for detail.

Arms – Right hand:

Starting from the fingers, cast on 6 sts in Wind Chime on a dpn.

Row 1-4: Work an i-cord for 4 rows.

Row 5: Cast off 3 sts, k to end. Leave the remaining sts waiting on a 3.5mm (US 4) straight needle.

Make 3 more fingers and place all 4 fingers together, wrong side facing.

Row 6: Cast on 12 sts, P across the 4 fingers. 24 sts

Row 7: [K2, k2tog, k2] 4 times. 20 sts

Row 8 and all even rows: P.

Leave these 20 sts waiting and make a 5th i-cord of 6 sts.

Row 1–4: Work the i-cord for 4 rows.

Row 9: K across the i-cord and then join and knit the 20 waiting sts. 26 sts

Row 10: P.

Row 11: K1, [k2, k2tog, k2] 4 times, k1. 22 sts

Row 13: K1, [k2, k2tog, k1] 4 times, k1. 18 sts

Row 14–39: St st 26 rows.

Row 40: Cast off 9 sts, p to end. 9 sts

Row 41: K2tog, k5, k2tog. 7 sts

Row 43: K2tog, k3, k2tog. 5 sts

Row 45: K2tog, k1, k2tog. 3 sts

Cast off and sew the bottom of the fingers to the palm on the hand and along the side edge. Stuff and attach to either side of the body.

Arm – Left hand:

Make 4 i-cords as for the right hand but place them on the straight needles with the right side facing and work as followed:

Row 6: P across all for fingers (12 sts), cast on 12 sts. 24 sts

Row 7: [K2, k2tog, k2] 4 times. 20 sts

Row 8 and all even rows: P.

Leave these 20 sts waiting and make a 5th i-cord of 6 sts.

Row 1–4: Work the i-cord for 4 rows.

Row 9: Join yarn to the 20 sts waiting. K20 and the knit across the 6 icord sts. 26 sts.

Row 10: P.

Row 11: K1, [k2, k2tog, k2] 4 times, k1. 22 sts

Row 13: K1, [k2, k2tog, k1] 4 times, k1. 18 sts

Row 14–40: St st 27 rows.

Row 41: Cast off 10 sts, k to the last 2 sts, k2tog. 7 sts

Row 43: K2tog, k3, k2tog. 5 sts

Row 45: K2tog, k1, k2tog. 3 sts

Cast off and sew as right hand.

Hairpiece:

Using Otter cast on 72 sts.

Row 1–10: St st 10 rows.

Row 11: [K3, k2tog, k3] 9 times. 63 sts

Row 12 and all even rows: P.

Row 13: [K2, k2tog, k3] 9 times. 54 sts

Row 15: [K2, k2tog, k2] 9 times. 45 sts

Row 17: [K1, k2tog, k2] 9 times. 36 sts

Row 19: [K1, k2tog, k1] 9 times. 27 sts

Row 21: [K2tog, k1] 9 times. 18 sts

Row 22: [P2tog] 9 times. 9 sts

Break yarn and thread through rem sts. Pull tight and fasten. Using mattress st sew along the side edge and position diagonal on the head. Attach with a running stitch. Using Otter sew a few lines for the fringe, starting from center of forehead outwards.

Crown:

Using Watermelon cast on 29 sts.

Row 1–4: G st 4 rows.

Row 5–10: Change to Crepe and st st 6 rows, starting with a k row.

Row 11: K1, *yo, k2tog; rep from * to end.

Row 12–18: St st 7 rows starting with a P row.

Row 19–22: Change to Watermelon and g st 4 rows.

Cast off. Fold the cast off edge towards the cast on edge and then join in a circle to create a crown.

Cut 60 strands of Otter measuring approximately 40 cm (15½ in). Place 3 strands of yarn in the center of the forehead. Using back stitch secure these strands in place. Place 3 more strands behind this and repeat all along the center of the head until you reach the middle of the back of the head. Next twist the yarn in the opposite direction of the yarn to separate the ply.

Sew the crown to the center of the head.

Dress:

Flower stitch:

With yarn in back, slip the next 5 sts to a cable needle purlwise dropping the extra wraps.

Wrap the yarn around the 5 sts on the cable needle twice. Then slip the 5 sts to the right-hand needle.

Using Watermelon cast on 97 sts.

Row 1: K.

Row 2: K1, * (knit the next stitch wrapping the yarn 3 times around the needle) 5 times, k 1; repeat from * to end.

Row 3: Purl 1, * flower stitch, p1; repeat from * to end.

Row 4: Knit.

Row 5–14: Change to Mulberry and st st 10 rows, starting with a k row.

Row 15: K1, [k14, k2tog] 6 times. 91 sts

Row 16–20: St st 5 rows.

Row 21: K1, [k13, k2tog] 6 times. 85 sts

Row 22–26: St st 5 rows.

Row 27: K1, [k12, k2tog] 6 times. 79 sts

Row 28–32: St st 5 rows.

Row 33: K1, [k11, k2tog] 6 times. 73 sts

Row 34–38: St st 5 rows.

Row 39: K1, [k10, k2tog] 6 times. 67 sts

Row 40–44: St st 5 rows.

Row 45: K1, [k9, k2tog] 6 times. 61 sts

Row 46–50: St st 5 rows.

Row 51: K1, [k8, k2tog] 6 times. 55 sts

Row 52–56: St st 5 rows.

Row 57: Change to Watermelon and K.

Row 58: K1, * (knit the next stitch wrapping the yarn 3 times around the needle) 5 times, k 1; repeat from * to end.

Row 59: Purl 1, * flower stitch, p1; repeat from * to end.

Row 60: Knit.

Row 61–67: Change to Mulberry and st st 7 rows, starting with a k row.

Row 68: P11, cast off 6 sts, p21, cast off 6 sts, p11. 43 sts

Row 69: Change to Watermelon and k11, cast on 12 sts, k21, cast on 12 sts, k to end. 67 sts.

Row 70: K1, * (knit the next stitch wrapping the yarn 3 times around the needle) 5 times, k 1; repeat from * to end.

Row 71: Purl 1, * flower stitch, p1; repeat from * to end.

Row 72: Cast off knitwise.

Using mattress sts sew along the side edge and dress your princess.

PUSS IN BOOTS

Puss in Boots is a very loyal creature who helped his master win the hand of a princess by using trickery and deceit. He insists on always looking his best and tried to teach his owner the same lesson.

YARN USED

- » Wendy Merino DK; 116m (380 ft) per 50 g (2 oz) ball; 100% Merino wool
- » 50 g (2 oz) Wendy Merino DK Funghi
- » 25 g (¾ oz) Wendy Merino DK Mulberry
- » 25 g (¾ oz) Wendy Merino DK Phlox
- » 25 g (¾ oz) Wendy Merino DK Jet
- » 25 g (¾ oz) Wendy Merino DK Otter
- » A small amount of green and pink for the facial features.

NEEDLES USED

- » 3.5mm (US 4) straight needles

OTHER SUPPLIES

- » Tapestry needle
- » Stuffing
- » Scissors

INSTRUCTIONS

Head:

Using Funghi cast on 16 sts.

Row 1: [K1, kfb] 8 times. 24 sts

Row 2 and all even rows: P.

Row 3: [K1, kfb, k1] 8 times. 32 sts

Row 5: [K2, kfb, k1] 8 times. 40 sts

Row 7: [K2, kfb, k2] 8 times. 48 sts

Row 9: [K3,kfb, k2] 8 times. 56 sts

Row 10-24: St st 15 rows starting wtih a P row.

Row 25: [K3, k2tog, k2] 8 times. 48 sts

Row 27: [K2, k2tog, k2] 8 times. 40 sts

Row 29: [K2, k2tog, k1] 8 times. 32 sts

Row 31: [K1, k2tog, k1] 8 times. 24 sts

Row 33: [K1, k2tog] 8 times. 16 sts

Row 35: [K2tog] 8 times. 8 sts

Break yarn and thread through rem. sts. Pull tight and fasten. Using mattress stitch sew along the side edge and stuff. For the eyes crochet a chain of 6 sts in green and join in the round using a slip st. Secure on the face and sew a line across for the eyes in Jet. Add two eyebrows above the eyes. For the nose, sew 3 horizontal lines in Watermelon decreasing in length. Then add a diagonal line on either side to tidy the edges. Create a vertical line downwards using 2 back sts and two diagonal lines either side for the mouth. Pinch the cheeks slightly to create a more cat like shape of the head.

Ears: (make two)

Using Funghi cast on 7 sts.

Row 1 and all odd rows: P.

Row 2: Kfb, k1, kfb, k1, kfb, k1, kfb. 11 sts

Row 4: Kfb, k3, kfb, k1, kfb, k3, kfb. 15 sts

Row 6: Kfb, k5, kfb, k1, kfb, k5, kfb. 19 sts

Row 8: Kfb, k7, kfb, k1, kfb, k7, kfb. 23 sts

Row 10: Kfb, k9, kfb, k1, kfb, k9, kfb. 27 sts

Row 11: P.

Cast off and fold in half. Sew along the side edge and attach to either side of the head.

Body:

Using Funghi cast on 8 sts.

Row 1: [Kfb] 8 times. 16 sts

Row 2 and all even rows: P.

Row 3: [K1, kfb] 8 times. 24 sts

Row 5: [K1, kfb, k1] 8 times. 32 sts

Row 7: [K2, kfb, k1] 8 times. 40 sts

Row 8–24: St st 17 rows.

Row 25: [K2, k2tog, k1] 8 times. 32 sts

Row 27: [K1, k2tog, k1] 8 times. 24 sts

Row 29: [K1, k2tog] 8 times. 16 sts

Row 31: [K2tog] 8 times. 8 sts

Break yarn and thread through rem. sts. Pull tight and fasten. Sew along the side edge using mattress stitch and stuff. Attach to the cast on edge of the head.

Arms: (make two)

Using Funghi cast on 6 sts.

Row 1 and all odd rows: P.

Row 2: Cast on 3 sts, k to end. 9 sts

Row 3: Cast on 3 sts, p to end. 12 sts

Row 4–5: Repeat rows 2-3: 18 sts

Row 6–19: St st 14 rows starting with a
k row.

Row 20: [K1, k2tog] 6 times. 12 sts

Row 22: [K2tog] 6 times. 6 sts

Break yarn and thread through rem. sts.
Pull tight and fasten. Sew along the side
edge using mattress stitch up to row 5 and
stuff. Attach to either side of the body.

Legs:

Using Jet cast on 18 sts.

Row 1 and all odd rows: P.

Row 2: K5, [kfb] 8 times, k5. 26 sts

Row 4: K5, [k1, kfb] 8 times, k5. 34 sts

Row 5–11: St st 7 rows.

Row 12: K5, [k1, k2tog] 8 times, k5. 26 sts

Row 14: K5, [k2tog] 8 times, k5. 18 sts

Row 15–27: Change to Funghi, st st 13 rows.

Cast off and sew along the side edge using
mattress sts. Stuff and attach to the body.

Boot cuffs:

Using Jet cast on 20 sts.

Row 1–6: St st 6 rows.

Cast off. Sew along the side edge using
mattress st and secure to the boots.

Tail:

Using Funghi cast on 10 sts.

Row 1–28: St st 28 rows.

Break yarn and thread through rem. Sts.
Pull tight and fasten. Sew the cast on
edge to the cast off edge to create a long
cylindrical shape.

Waistcoat:

Using Phlox cast on 44 sts.

Row 1–10: St st 10 rows starting with a k row.

Row 11: K2tog, k9, leaving the rem. sts on a
holding needle. 10 sts

Row 12 and all even rows: P.

Row 13: K2tog, k8. 9 sts

Row 15: K2tog, k7. 8 sts

Row 17: K2tog. K6. 7 sts

Row 18–20: St st 3 rows.

Cast off and join yarn to the next 22 sts on
the holding needle, leaving the last 11 sts
waiting.

Row 11–20: st st 10 rows.

Cast off.

Join yarn to the last 11 sts.

Row 11: K9, k2tog. 10 sts

Row 12 and all even rows: P.

Row 13: K8, k2tog. 9 sts

Row 15: K7, k2tog. 8 sts

Row 17: K6, k2tog. 7 sts

Row 18–20: St st 3 rows.

Cast off. Sew shoulder parts together using
mattress st.

Trousers:

Using Mulberry cast on 20 sts.

Row 1: [K2, kfb, k2] 4 times. 24 sts

Row 2-8: st st 7 rows.

Break yarn and knit a second trouser leg.

Row 9: K across both legs. 48 sts

Row 10-24: St st 15 rows.

Row 25: [K2, k2tog, k2] 8 times. 40 sts

Cast off. Using mattress sts sew both trouser legs together and then sew the part of the trousers halfway up. Position on the cat and pin the tail in place. Continue to sew the trousers to the top, leaving a gap for the tail. Secure the tail to the body.

Hat:

Using Otter cast on 40 sts

Row 1 and all odd rows: P.

Row 2: [K2, kfb, k2] 8 times. 48 sts

Row 4: [K2, kfb, k3] 8 times. 56 sts

Row 6: [K3, kfb, k3] 8 times. 64 sts

Row 8: [K3, kfb, k4] 8 times. 72 sts

Row 10: [K4, kfb, k4] 8 times. 80 sts

Row 12: [K4, k2tog, k4] 8 times. 72 sts

Row 14: [K4, k2tog, k3] 8 times. 64 sts

Row 16: [K3, k2tog, k3] 8 times. 56 sts

Row 18: [K3, k2tog, k2] 8 times. 48 sts

Row 20: [K2, k2tog, k2] 8 times. 40 sts

Rw 21-29: St st 9 rows.

Row 30: [K2, k2tog, k1] 8 times. 32 sts

Row 32: [K1, k2tog, k1] 8 times. 24 sts

Row 34: [K1, k2tog] 8 times. 16 sts

Row 36: [K2tog] 8 times. 8 sts

Break yarn and thread through rem. sts. Pull tight and fasten. Sew along the side edge using mattress sts. Fold the cast on edge inwards and secure with running sts. Fold two sides of the rim to the side of the hat and secure with sts.

DWARF

Dwarves are often found near mountain sides, mining various caves looking for treasure. These little creatures love anything shiny and make excellent treasure boxes. Each dwarf is made out of an empty Kinder Egg shell, making them excellent hiding places for trinkets. They are great for stash busting as they require only limited amount of yarn.

YARN USED

» Wendy Merino DK; 116m (380 ft) per 50 g (2 oz) ball; 100% Merino wool
» Small amount of Wind Chime (nose) and Jet (shoes)
» 10 g (½ oz) Wendy Merino DK Smoke (beard)
» 10 g (½ oz) Wendy Merino DK Persian Red, Blue Lagoon, Pacific, Phlox, Mulberry, Fennel, Spruce

NEEDLES USED

» 3.5mm (US 4) straight needles

OTHER SUPPLIES

» Tapestry needle
» Stuffing
» Crochet hook
» 7 empty Kinder Egg shells

INSTRUCTIONS

Body:

Using Blue lagoon cast on 28 sts.

Row 1–8: St st 8 rows.

Row 9: [K1, k2tog, k1] 7 times. 21 sts

Row 10: P.

Row 11: [K1, k2tog] 7 times. 14 sts

Row 12: [P2tog] 7 times. 7 sts

Break yarn and thread through rem. Sts. Pull tight and fasten. Sew along the side edge using mattress sts.

Feet: (make two)

Using Jet cast on 12 sts.

Row 1–4: St st 4 rows.

Row 5: [K2tog] 6 times.

Break yarn and thread through rem. Sts. Pull tight and fasten. Sew along the side edge using mattress sts. Attach to the bottom of the body.

Hat:

Using Persian Red cast on 28 sts.

Row 1–4: G st 4 rows.

Row 5–8: St st 4 rows starting with a k row.

Row 9: k2tog, k to last 2 sts, k2tog. 26 sts

Row 10 and all even rows: P.

Row 11–14: Repeat rows 9–10 twice. 22 sts

Row 15: K1, [k2, k2tog, k1] 4 times, k1. 18 sts

Row 17: K1, [k1, k2tog, k1] 4 times, k1. 14 sts

Row 19: K1, [k1, k2tog] 4 times, k1. 10 sts

Row 21: K1, [k2tog] 4 times, k1. 6 sts

Row 22: P.

Break yarn and thread through rem. Sts. Pull tight and fasten. Sew along the side edge using mattress sts. Using running sts, secure the back of the head to the back of the body, overlapping slightly.

Nose:

Using Wind Chime cast on 10 sts.

Row 1–4: St st 4 rows.

Row 5: [K2tog] 5 times. 5 sts

Break yarn and thread through rem. Sts. Pull tight and fasten. Sew along the side edge using mattress sts. Sew to the center of the hat.

Beard:

Cut approximately 14 strands of Silver, measuring 10 cm (4 in) long. Insert the crochet hook to the inside of the hat, 2 cm (¾ in) away from the nose, and pull a strand of Silver halfway through. Insert both ends of the strand through the loop and pull to secure. Repeat in a straight line across the nose. Untwist the strands to create a waved effect. Trim as desired.

Place an empty Kinder Egg shell inside the dwarf, the smallest part for the hat and the biggest part for the body. Apply some super glue to secure the yarn to the egg.

Repeat this with other yarn combinations
until all seven dwarves are completed.

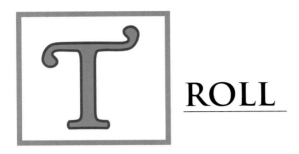

TROLL

Trolls are peculiar little creatures who are found in various different folklores, sometimes good, sometimes evil but often presented with big noses and huge flappy ears. They are said to live in the woods or in caves along the mountain side.

YARN USED

» Wendy Merino DK; 116m (380 ft) per 50 g (2 oz) ball; 100% Merino wool

» 100 g (3½ oz) Wendy Merino DK Latte

» 50 g (2 oz) Wendy Merino DK Otter

NEEDLES USED

» 3.5mm (US 4) straight needles

» 2, 3.5mm (US 4) double pointed needles

OTHER SUPPLIES

» Tapestry needle

» Stuffing

» One small button

INSTRUCTIONS

Body:

Using Latte cast on 24 sts.

Row 1–4: St st 4 rows, starting with a k row.

Row 5: [K1, kfb, k1] 8 times. 32 sts

Row 6–8: St st 3 rows.

Row 9: [K2, kfb, k1] 8 times. 40 sts

Row 10–12: St st 3 rows.

Row 13: [K2, kfb, k2] 8 times. 48 sts

Row 14–16: St st 3 rows.

Row 17: [K3, kfb, k2] 8 times. 56 sts

Row 18–24: St st 7 rows.

Row 25: [K3, k2tog, k2] 8 times. 48 sts

Row 26 and all even rows: P.

Row 27: [K2, k2tog, k2] 8 times. 40 sts

Row 29: [K2, k2tog, k1] 8 times. 32 sts

Row 31: [K1, k2tog, k1] 8 times. 24 sts

Row 33: [K1, k2tog] 8 times. 16 sts

Row 34: [P2tog] 8 times. 8 sts

Break yarn and thread through rem. sts. Pull tight and fasten. Using mattress stitch sew along the side edge and stuff, leaving the cast on edge open.

Legs: (make two)

Starting from the bottom of the foot cast on 19 sts using Latte.

Row 1 and all odd rows: Purl.

Row 2: K1, [kfb] 16 times, k2. 35 sts

Rows 3–11: Work in St st for 9 rows.

Row 12: K4, [k2tog] 13 times, k5. 22 sts

Row 14: K3, [k2tog] 8 times, k3. 14 sts

Rows 15–35: St st for 21 rows starting with a p row.

Row 36: K2, [k2tog] twice, k2, [k2tog] twice, k2. 10 sts

Cast off loosely. Sew up the bottom of the foot first and continue along the back edge, leaving the cast off edge open. Stuff and knit a second identical leg. Sew the legs to the body.

Head:

Using Latte cast on 16 sts.

Row 1 and all odd rows: P.

Row 2: [K1, kfb] 8 times. 24 sts

Row 4: [K1, kfb, k1] 8 times. 32 sts

Row 6: [K2, kfb, k1] 8 times. 40 sts

Row 8: [k2, kfb, k2] 8 times. 48 sts

Row 10: [K3, kfb, k2] 8 times. 56 sts

Row 12: [K3, kfb, k3] 8 times. 64 sts

Row 14: [K4, kfb, k3] 8 times. 72 sts

Row 15–33: St st 19 rows.

Row 34: [K4, k2tog, k3] 8 times. 64 sts

Row 36: [K3, k2tog, k3] 8 times. 56 sts

Row 38: [K3, k2tog, k2] 8 times. 48 sts

Row 40: [K2, k2tog, k2] 8 times. 40 sts

Row 42: [K2, k2tog, k1] 8 times. 32 sts

Row 44: [K1, k2tog, k1] 8 times. 24 sts

Row 46: [K1, k2tog] 8 times. 16 sts

Row 45: [P2tog] 8 times. 8 sts

Break yarn and thread through rem. sts. Pull tight and fasten. Sew along the side edge and stuff. Attach the body to the head.

Ears: (Make 2)

Using Latte cast on 17 sts.

Row 1: Kfb, k6, kfb, k1, kfb, k6, kfb. 21 sts

Row 2 and all even rows: P.

Row 3: Kfb, k8, kfb, k1, kfb, k8, kfb. 25 sts

Row 5: [Kfb] twice, k8, [kfb] twice, k1, [kfb] twice, k8, [kfb] twice. 33 sts

Row 7: [Kfb] twice, k12, [kfb] twice, k1, [kfb] twice, k12, [kfb] twice. 41 sts

Row 9: [Kfb] twice, k16, [kfb] twice, k1, [kfb] twice, k16, [kfb] twice. 49 sts

Row 10-20: St st 11 rows.

Row 21: K2tog, k18, [k2tog] twice, k1, [k2tog] twice, k18, k2tog. 43 sts

Row 22-24: St st 3 rows.

Row 25: K2tog, k15, [k2tog] twice, k1, [k2tog] twice, k15, k2tog. 37 sts

Row 26-28: St st 3 rows.

Row 29: K2tog, k12, [k2tog] twice, k1, [k2tog] twice, k12, k2tog. 31 sts

Row 30-32: St st 3 rows.

Row 33: K2tog, k9, [k2tog] twice, k1, [k2tog] twice, k9, k2tog. 25 sts

Row 34-36: St st 3 rows.

Row 37: K2tog, k6, [k2tog] twice, k1, [k2tog] twice, k6, k2tog. 19 sts

Row 38-40: St st 3 rows.

Row 41: K2tog, k3, [k2tog] twice, k1, [k2tog] twice, k3, k2tog. 13 sts

Row 42-44: St st 3 rows.

Row 45: [K2tog] 3 times, k1, [k2tog] 3 times. 7 sts

Row 46-48: St st 3 rows.

Row 49: K2tog, k3, k2tog. 5 sts

Row 51: K2tog, k1, k2tog. 3 sts

Row 53: K3tog. 1 sts

Break yarn and thread through rem. sts. Pull tight and fasten. Using mattress stitch sew along the side edge and close the cast on edge. Attach to either side of the head with the cast on edge.

Nose:

Using Latte cast on 32 sts.

Row 1-6: St st 6 rows starting with a k row.

Row 7: [K1, k2tog, k1] 8 times. 24 sts

Row 8: P.

Row 9: [K1, k2tog] 8 times. 16 sts

Row 10: [P2tog] 8 times. 8 sts

Break yarn and thread through rem. Sts. Pull tight and fasten. Using mattress st sew along the side edge and stuff. Attach to the face. For the eyes, create two diagonal lines using black.

Arm – Right hand:

Starting from the fingers and cast on 6 sts in MC1 on a dpn.

Row 1-4: Work an i-cord for 4 rows.

Row 5: Cast off 3 sts, k to end. Leave the remaining sts waiting on a 3.5mm (US 4) straight needle.

Make 2 more fingers and place all 3 fingers together with the wrong side facing.

Row 6: Cast on and p 9 sts, p across the 3 fingers. 18 sts.

Row 7: [K2, k2tog, k2] 3 times. 15 sts

Row 8 and all even rows: P.

Leave these 15 sts waiting and make a 4th i-cord of 6 sts.

Row 1–4: Work the i-cord for 4 rows.

Row 9: Join the i-cord to the beginning of the 15 waiting sts and k to end. 21 sts

Row 10: P.

Row 11: K1, [k2, k2tog, k2] 3 times, k2. 18 sts

Row 13: K1, [k2, k2tog, k1] 3 times, k2. 15 sts

Row 14–35: St st 22 rows.

Row 36: Cast off 8 sts, p to end. 7 sts

Row 37: K2tog, k3, k2tog. 5 sts

Row 39: K2tog, k1, k2tog. 3 sts

Cast off and sew the bottom of the fingers to the palm on the hand and along the side edge. Stuff and attach to either side of the body.

Arm – Left hand:

Make 3 i-cords as for the right hand but place them on the straight needles with the right side facing and work as followed:

Row 6: P9, cast on 9 sts. 18 sts

Row 7: [K2, k2tog, k2] 3 times. 15 sts

Row 8 and all even rows: P.

Leave these 15 sts waiting and make a 4th i-cord of 6 sts.

Row 1–4: Work the i-cord for 4 rows.

Row 9: Join yarn to the 15 sts waiting. K15 and then knit across the 6 i-cord sts. 21 sts.

Row 10: P.

Row 11: K1, [k2, k2tog, k2] 3 times, k2. 18 sts

Row 13: K1, [k2, k2tog, k1] 3 times, k2. 15 sts

Row 14–35: St st 22 rows.

Row 36: Cast off 8 sts, p to end. 7 sts

Row 37: K2tog, k3, k2tog. 5 sts

Row 39: K2tog, k1, k2tog. 3 sts

Cast off and sew as right hand.

Dungarees:

Using Otter cast on 18 sts.

Row 1: [K1, kfb] 9 times. 27 sts

Row 2–4: St st 3 rows starting with a p row.

Row 5: [K1, kfb, k1] 9 times. 36 sts

Row 6–12: St st 7 rows.

Break yarn and place rem sts on a holder. Knit a second trouser leg identically.

Row 13: K across 36 sts then k across 36 sts on holding needle. 72 sts

Row 14–40: St st 27 rows.

Row 41: K1 [k4, k2tog, k4] 7 times, k1. 65 sts

Row 42: P.

Row 43: K1, [k3, k2tog, k4] 7 times, k1. 58 sts

Cast off. Using mattress sts sew along the trouser legs first and then continue along the back of the trousers.

Strap:

Using Otter cast on 30 sts.

Row 1 and all odd rows: P.

Row 2: K2tog, yo, k to end.

Row 3: P.

Cast off.

Secure the strap to the back of the trousers. Position the strap diagonally to the front of the body and secure a button to the front of the trousers.

W AND

Every self-respecting fairy princess needs a magic wand to perform good (or evil) acts in their own fairy tales. To keep the wand nice and straight I used a chop stick, however this could also be replaced by a straw or a pipe cleaner.

YARN USED

» Wendy Merino DK; 116m (380 ft) per 50 g (2 oz) ball; 100% Merino wool
» 25 g (¾ oz) Wendy Merino DK Seaspray
» 25 g (¾ oz) Wendy Merino DK Phlox
» Three small amounts of various shades of blue or green.

NEEDLES USED

» 3.5mm (US 4) straight needles

OTHER SUPPLIES

» Tapestry needle
» Stuffing
» Chop sticks

INSTRUCTIONS

Wand:

Using Seaspray create an i-cord of 4 sts measuring the length of your chopstick. Secure the sts and insert your chopstick through the middle.

Star:

Cast on 3 sts using Phlox for the points.

Row 1 and all odd rows: P

Row 2: kfb, k1, kfb. 5 sts

Row 4: kfb, k3, kfb. 7 sts

Row 6: kfb, k5, kfb. 9 sts

Row 8: kfb, k7, kfb. 11 sts

Row 10: kfb, k9, kfb. 13 sts

Row 12: kfb, k11, kfb . 15 sts

Break yarn and leave the rem. 15 sts on a holding needle. Knit another 4 points but do not break the yarn on the last point.

Row 13: Pfb twice, p13, join and p across the other 3 points, join the last point, p to the last 2 sts, pfb twice. 79 sts

Row 14: K2, [ssk, k11, k2tog] 5 times, k2. 69 sts

Row 16: K2, [ssk, k9, k2tog] 5 times, k2. 59 sts

Row 18: K2, [ssk, k7, k2tog] 5 times, k2. 49 sts

Row 20: K2, [ssk, k5, k2tog] 5 times, k2. 39 sts

Row 22: K2, [ssk, k3, k2tog] 5 times, k2. 29 sts

Row 24: K2, [ssk, k1, k2tog] 5 times, k2. 19 sts

Row 25: P1, [p2tog] 9 times. 10 sts.

Break yarn and thread through rem. sts. Pull tight and fasten. Sew along the side edge and knit a second star. Join both stars along the side edge and stuff. Attach to the wand before closing up.

Tassels: (make 3)

Using different shades of blue, cast on 36 sts, then cast off knitwise.

Sew the tassels to the bottom of the star.

WITCH

Witches are very powerful magical creatures who use their powers for good or evil. They love to play tricks on people and cook up all sorts of potions in their cauldrons.

YARN USED

» Wendy Merino DK; 116m (380 ft) per 50 g (2 oz) ball; 100% Merino wool
» 50 g (2 oz) Wendy Merino DK Jet
» 50 g (2 oz) Wendy Merino DK Wind Chime
» 25 g (¾ oz) Wendy Merino DK Fennel
» 50 g (2 oz) Wendy Merino DK Crepe
» 50 g (2 oz) Wendy Merino DK blue

NEEDLES USED

» 3.5mm (US 4) straight needles
» 3.5 mm (US 4) double pointed needles

OTHER SUPPLIES

» Tapestry needle
» Stuffing

INSTRUCTIONS

Legs: (make two)

Starting from the bottom of the foot cast on 22 sts using Jet.

Row 1 and all odd rows: Purl.

Row 2: K1, [kfb] 20 times, k1. 42 sts

Rows 3–17: Work in St st for 15 rows.

Row 18: K7, [k2tog] 14 times, k7. 28 sts

Row 20: K7, [k2tog] 7 times, k7. 21 sts

Rows 21–63: Change to Fennel and work 4 rows Fennel, 4 rows crepe in st st for 43 rows.

Row 64: K4, [k2tog] twice, k5, [k2tog] twice, k4. 17 sts

Cast off loosely. Sew up the bottom of the foot first and continue along the back edge, leaving the cast off edge open. Stuff and knit a second identical leg.

Body:

Starting at the bottom, cast on 14 sts using Wind Chime.

Rows 1–2: Work in St st for 2 rows.

Row 3: [Kfb] 14 times. 28 sts

Row 4 and all even rows: P.

Row 5: [Kfb] 28 times. 56 sts

Rows 6–30: Work in St st for 25 rows.

Row 31: [K2tog] 28 times. 28 sts

Rows 32–36: Work in St st for 5 rows.

Row 37: [K2tog] 14 times. 14 sts

Row 38 and all even rows: P.

Row 39: [Kfb] 14 times. 28 sts

Row 41: [K1, kfb] 14 times. 42 sts

Row 43: [K1, kfb, k1] 14 times. 56 sts

Row 45: [K2, kfb, k1] 14 times. 70 sts

Row 46–64: St st 19 sts.

Row 65: [K2, k2tog, k1] 14 times. 56 sts

Row 67: [K1, k2tog, k1] 14 times. 42 sts

Row 69: [K1, k2tog] 14 times. 28 sts

Row 71: [K2tog] 14 times. 14 sts

Row 72: [P2tog] 7 times. 7 sts

Break yarn and draw through rem sts, pull tight and fasten. Sew along the back, leaving the cast on edge open for stuffing.

Arm – Right hand:

Starting from the fingers, cast on 6 sts in Wind Chime on a dpn.

Row 1–4: Work an i-cord for 4 rows.

Row 5: Cast off 3 sts, k to end. Leave the remaining sts waiting on a 3.5mm (US 4) straight needle.

Make 3 more fingers and place all 4 fingers together with the wrong side facing.

Row 6: Cast on 12 sts, p across the 4 fingers. 24 sts

Row 7: [K2, k2tog, k2] 4 times. 20 sts

Row 8 and all even rows: P.

Leave these 20 sts waiting and make a 5th i-cord of 6 sts.

Row 1–4: Work the i-cord for 4 rows.

Row 9: K across the i-cord, then join and k the 20 waiting sts. 26 sts

Row 10: P.

Row 11: K1, [k2, k2tog, k2] 4 times, k1. 22 sts
Row 13: K1, [k2, k2tog, k1] 4 times, k1. 18 sts
Row 14–39: St st 26 rows.
Row 40: Cast off 9 sts, p to end. 9 sts
Row 41: K2tog, k5, k2tog. 7 sts
Row 43: K2tog, k3, k2tog. 5 sts
Row 45: K2tog, k1, k2tog. 3 sts
Cast off and sew the bottom of the fingers to the palm of the hand and along the side edge. Stuff and attach to either side of the body.

Arm – Left hand:
Make 4 i-cords as for the right hand but place them on the straight needles with the right side facing and work as follows:
Row 6: P 12, cast on 12 sts. 24 sts
Row 7: [K2, k2tog, k2] 4 times. 20 sts
Row 8 and all even rows: P.
Leave these 20 sts waiting and make a 5th i-cord of 6 sts.
Row 1–4: Work the i-cord for 4 rows.
Row 9: Join yarn to the 20 sts waiting. K20 and the knit across the 6 icord sts. 26 sts.
Row 10: P.
Row 11: K1, [k2, k2tog, k2] 4 times, k1. 22 sts
Row 13: K1, [k2, k2tog, k1] 4 times, k1. 18 sts
Row 14–40: St st 27 rows.
Row 41: Cast off 10 sts, k6, k2tog. 7 sts
Row 43: K2tog, k3, k2tog. 5 sts
Row 45: K2tog, k1, k2tog. 3 sts

Cast off and sew as right hand.

Hairpiece:
Using Crepe cast on 72 sts.
Row 1–10: St st 10 rows.
Row 11: [K3, k2tog, k3] 9 times. 63 sts
Row 12 and all even rows: P.
Row 13: [K2, k2tog, k3] 9 times. 54 sts
Row 15: [K2, k2tog, k2] 9 times. 45 sts
Row 17: [K1, k2tog, k2] 9 times. 36 sts
Row 19: [K1, k2tog, k1] 9 times. 27 sts
Row 21: [K2tog, k1] 9 times. 18 sts
Row 22: [P2tog] 9 times. 9 sts
Break yarn and thread through rem sts. Pull tight and fasten. Using mattress stitch sew along the side edge and position diagonal on the head. Attach with a running stitch.

Cut the remaining Crepe yarn into strands of 50 cm (19½ in) long. Place three strands of Crepe in the middle of the scalp and secure using a backstitch. Repeat along the length of the head. Next fold a strand of hair in half, insert the crochet hook into the edge of the hair cap, hook the middle of the strand over the hook, pull back and then insert both ends of the strand through the loop created. Pull tight to secure. Continue to do this all along the edge of the hair cap. Take a section of hair from either side of the head, pull them towards the back and tie in a loose knot.

Dress:

Using Sloe cast on 100 sts.

Row 1 and all odd rows: Purl.

Row 2: K2tog, *k5, yo, k1, yo, k2, sl 1, k2tog, psso; rep from * until the last 10 sts, k5, yo, k1, yo, k2, ssk.

Row 4: K2tog, *k4, yo, k3, yo, k1, sl 1, k2tog, psso; rep from *, until the last 10 sts, k4, yo, k3, yo, k1, ssk.

Row 6: K2tog, *k3, yo, k5, yo, sl 1, k2tog, psso; rep from *, until the last 10 sts, k3, yo, k5, yo, k1, ssk.

Row 8: K2tog, *k2, yo, k1, yo, k5, sl 1, k2tog, psso; rep from *, until the last 10 sts, k2, yo, k1, yo, k5, ssk.

Row 10: K2tog, *k1, yo, k3, yo, k4, sl 1, k2tog, psso; rep from *, until the last 10 sts, k1, yo, k3, yo, k4, ssk.

Row 12: K2tog, * yo, k5, yo, k3, sl 1, k2tog, psso; rep from *, until the last 10 sts, yo, k5, yo, k3, ssk.

Row 13–36: Repeat rows 1–12.

Row 38: [K2, k2tog, k1] 20 times. 80 sts

Row 40: [K1, k2tog, k1] 20 times. 60 sts

Row 42: [K6, k2tog, k7] 4 times. 56 sts

Row 43–49: St st 7 rows.

Row 50: K13, cast off 4, k22, cast off 4, k13. Continue on the first 13 sts, leaving the other sts waiting.

Row 51: Purl across the first 13 sts, leaving the remaining sts waiting.

Row 52: K2tog, k to end. 12 sts

Row 53–56: St st 4 rows.

Row 57: Cast off 6 sts, p to end. 6 sts

Row 58–61: St st 4 rows.

Cast off.

Join yarn to the next 22 sts waiting.

Row 51: P.

Row 52: K2tog, k18, k2tog. 20 sts

Row 53–56: St st 4 rows.

Row 57: P6, cast off 8 sts, p6. Continue working on the first 6 sts:

Row 58–61: St st 4 rows.

Cast off.

Repeat rows 58–61 for the next 6 sts.

Join yarn to the next 13 sts.

Row 51: P.

Row 52: K11, k2tog. 12 sts

Row 53–57: St st 5 rows.

Row 58: Cast off 6 sts, k to end. 6 sts

Row 59–61: St st 3 rows.

Cast off.

Sew the shoulder parts together and then starting from the bottom sew along the side edge, leaving the last 2 cm (¾ in) open. Attach a small button on one side and make a crochet chain of 8 sts and secure this on the other side as a loop.

Sleeves:

Using Sloe cast on 12 sts.

Row 1 and all odd rows: P.

Row 2: Cast on 3 sts, k to end. 15 sts

Row 3: Cast on 3 sts, p to end. 18 sts

Row 4–5: Repeat rows 1–2. 24 sts

Row 6: Kfb, k22. Kfb. 26 sts

Row 8: Kfb, k24, kfb. 28 sts

Row 10: Kfb, k26, kfb. 30 sts

Row 12: Kfb, k28, kfb. 32 sts

Row 14: Kfb, k30, kfb. 34 sts

Row 16: Kfb, k32, kfb. 36 sts

Row 18: Kfb, k34, kfb. 38 sts

Row 20: Kfb, k36, kfb. 40 sts

Row 22: Kfb, k38, kfb. 42 sts

Row 24: Kfb, k40, kfb. 44 sts

Cast off and sew along the side edge. Attach cast on edge to the arm opening in the dress.

Hat rim:

Using Jet cast on 144 sts.

Row 1 and all odd rows: P.

Row 2: [K8, k2tog, k8] 8 times. 136 sts

Row 4: [K8, k2tog, k7] 8 times. 128 sts

Row 6: [K7, k2tog, k7] 8 times. 120 sts

Row 8: [K7, k2tog, k6] 8 times. 112 sts

Row 10: [K6, k2tog, k6] 8 times. 104 sts

Row 12: [K6, k2tog, k5] 8 times. 96 sts

Row 14: [K5, k2tog, k5] 8 times. 88 sts

Row 16: [K5, k2tog, k4] 8 times. 80 sts

Cast off. Sew along the side edge.

Hat:

Cast on 80 sts using Jet.

Row 1: [K9, k2tog, k9] 4 times. 76 sts

Row 2–4: St st 3 rows.

Row 5: [K9, k2tog, k8] 4 times. 72 sts

Row 6–8: St st 3 rows.

Row 9: [K8, kfb, k8] 4 times. 68 sts

Row 10–12: St st 3 rows.

Row 13: [K8, k2tog, k7] 4 times. 64 sts

Row 14–16: St st 3 rows.

Row 17: [K7, k2tog, k7] 4 times. 60 sts

Row 18–20: St st 3 rows.

Row 21: [K7, k2tog, k6] 4 times. 56 sts

Row 22–24: St st 3 rows.

Row 25: [K6, k2tog, k6] 4 times. 52 sts

Row 26–28: St st 3 rows.

Row 29: [K6, k2tog, k5] 4 times. 48 sts

Row 30–32: St st 3 rows.

Row 33: [K5, k2tog, k5] 4 times. 44 sts

Row 34–36: St st 3 rows.

Row 37: [K5, k2tog, k4] 4 times. 40 sts

Row 38–40: St st 3 rows.

Row 41: [K4, k2tog, k4] 4 times. 36 sts

Row 42–44: St st 3 rows.

Row 45: [K4, k2tog, k3] 4 times. 32 sts

Row 46–48: St st 3 rows.

Row 49: [K3, k2tog, k3] 4 times. 28 sts

Row 50–52: St st 3 rows.

Row 53: [K3, k2tog, k2] 4 times. 24 sts

Row 54–56: St st 3 rows.

Row 57: [K2, k2tog, k2] 4 times. 20 sts

Row 58–60: St st 3 rows.

Row 61: [K2, k2tog, k1] 4 times. 16 sts

Row 62–64: St st 3 rows.

Row 65: [K1, k2tog, k1] 4 times. 12 sts

Row 66–68: St st 3 rows.

Row 69: [K1, k2tog] 4 times. 8 sts

Row 70–72: St st 3 rows.

Row 73: [K2tog] 4 times. 4 sts

Cast off and sew along the side edge.
Attach the cast on edge to the cast off edge
of the rim.

WOODLAND FAERIES

Faeries are little winged creatures who live in all parts of the world. These particular faeries live in the woods and are the guardians of all the living creatures and plants there.

YARN USED

» Wendy Merino DK; 116m (380 ft) per 50 g (2 oz) ball; 100% Merino wool
» 50 g (2 oz) Wendy Merino DK Wind Chime
» 25g (¾ oz) Wendy Merino DK Cloud dancer
» 50g (2 oz) Wendy Merino DK Crepe
» 25g (¾ oz) Wendy Merino DK Jet
» 25g (¾ oz) Wendy Merino DK Otter
» 25g (¾ oz) Wendy Merino DK Seaspray
» 25g (¾ oz) Wendy Merino DK Mullberry
» 25g (¾ oz) Wendy Merino DK Wood Violet
» 10g (½ oz) Wendy Merino DK Fennel

NEEDLES USED

» 3.5mm (US 4) straight needles

OTHER SUPPLIES

» Tapestry needle
» Stuffing
» Crochet hook

INSTRUCTIONS

Head and body:

Cast on 11 sts in Wind Chime.

Row 1: [kfb] 11 times. 22 sts

Row 2-4: St st 3 rows.

Row 5: [K1, kfb] 11 times. 33 sts

Row 6-8: St st 3 rows.

Row 9: [K1, kfb, k1] 11 times. 44 sts

Row 10-16: St st 7 rows.

Row 17: [K1, k2tog, k1] 11 times. 33 sts

Row 18-20: St st 3 rows.

Row 21: [K1, k2tog] 11 times. 22 sts

Row 22 and all even rows: P.

Row 23: [k2tog] 11 times. 11 sts

Row 25: K1, [k2tog] 5 times. 6 sts

Row 26: Change to Crepe/Seaspray or Wood Violet and p to end.

Row 27: K1, [kfb] 4 times, k1. 10 sts

Row 29: [Kfb] 10 times. 20 sts

Row 31: [K1, kfb] 10 times. 30 sts

Row 32-40: St st 9 rows.

Row 41: [K1, k2tog] 11 times. 20 sts

Row 43: [K2tog] 10 times. 10sts

Row 44: [P2tog] 5 times. 5 sts

Break yarn and thread through the remaining stitches. Pull tight and fasten. Sew along the edge using mattress stitch and leave the top part open for stuffing. Using some scrap yarn make two French knots for the eyes.

Arms: (make 2)

Cast on 6 sts from top of arm in Wind Chime.

Row 1 and all odd rows: P.

Row 2-3: Cast on 2 st at the beginning of the next 2 rows. 10 sts

Row 4-13: St st 10 rows.

Row 14: [K2tog] 5 times. 5 sts

Break yarn and thread through the remaining stitches. Pull tight and fasten. Sew along the edge using mattress stitch up to row 3. Attach to either side of the body.

Legs: (make 2)

Starting from the bottom of the foot, cast on 11 st in Crepe/Seaspray or Wood Violet.

Row 1: K.

Row 2: K2 [kfb] 8 times, k1. 19 sts

Row 3-6: G st 4 rows.

Row 7: K2, [K2tog, k1] 5 times, k2. 14 sts

Row 8: K3, [k2tog] 4 times, k3. 10sts

Row 9-18: Change to Wind Chime and st st 10 rows, starting with a k row.

Cast off. Using mattress stitch sew the bottom of the foot and along the back edge, leaving the top part open for filling and connecting to the body.

Ears: (make 2)

Using Wind Chime cast on 7 sts.

Row 1: [Kfb, k1] 3 times, kfb. 11 sts

Row 2 and all even rows: P.

Row 3: [Kfb] twice, k2, kfb, k1, kfb, k2, [kfb] twice. 17 sts

Row 5: [K2tog] twice, k2, k2tog, k1, k2tog

k2, [k2tog] twice. 11 sts

Row 7: [K2tog] twice, k3, [k2tog] twice. 7 sts

Row 8: P2tog, p3, p2tog. 5 sts

Row 9: K2tog, k1, k2tog. 3 sts

Cast off and fold in half. Sew along the edge and attach to the side of the head after adding hair.

Wings: (make 4)

Using Cloud Dancer cast on 6 sts.

Row 1: [Kfb, k1, kfb] twice. 10 sts

Row 2–4: St st 3 rows.

Row 5: [Kfb, k3, kfb] twice. 14 sts

Row 6–8: St st 3 rows.

Row 9: [Kfb, k5, kfb] twice. 18 sts

Row 10–12: St st 3 rows.

Row 13: [K2tog, k5, k2tog] twice. 14 sts

Row 14: P.

Row 15: [K2tog, k3, k2tog] twice. 10 sts

Row 16: P.

Row 17: [K2tog, k1, k2tog] twice. 6 sts

Break yarn and thread through remaining stitches. Sew along the side edge and cast on edge. Position the wings two by two along the back of the pixie and sew in place.

Dress option 1:

Using Mulberry, cast on 31 sts.

Row 1: K1, *yo, sl1, k1, psso, k1, k2tog, yo, k1; rep. from * to end.

Row 2: P.

Row 3: K2, *yo, sl1, k2tog, psso, yo, k3; rep,

from * to last 5 sts, yo, sl1, k2tog, psso, yo, k2.

Row 4: P.

Row 5–12: repeat rows 1–4.

Row 13–15: Change to Wood Violet and work 3 rows in G st.

Cast off. Using mattress st sew along the side edge and secure to the body.

Dress option 2:

Using Seaspray cast on 30 sts.

Row 1–2: G st 2 rows.

Row 3: Change to Crepe and K1, [k1, kfb, k2] 7 times, k1. 37 sts

Row 4–6: St st 3 rows.

Row 7–8: Change to Seaspray and G st 2 rows.

Row 9: Change to Crepe and K1, [k2, kfb, k2] 7 times, k1. 44 sts

Row 10–12: St st 3 rows.

Row 13–14: Change to Seaspray and g st 2 rows.

Row 15: Change to Crepe and K1, [k2, kfb, k3] 7 times, k1. 51 sts

Row 16–18: St st 3 rows.

Row 19–20: Change to Seaspray and g st 2 rows.

Cast off. Using mattress st sew along the side edge and secure to the body.

Dress option 3:

Using Fennel cast on 58 sts.

Row 1-4: St st 4 rows starting with a k row.

Row 5: K1, *k2tog, yo; rep from * to last sts, k1.

Row 6-9: St st 4 rows Seaspray starting with a p row.

Row 10–26: St st 16 rows.

Row 27: *K2tog; rep from * to end. 29 sts
Cast off. Fold the cast off edge inwards and secure with running sts. Using mattress sts sew along the side edge and attach to the body.

Hair:

Using Crepe/Jet or Otter cast on 44 sts.

Row 1-8: St st 8 rows.

Row 9: K2, [k2, k2tog, k1] 8 times, k2. 36 sts

Row 10 and all even rows: P.

Row 11: K2, [k1, k2tog, k1] 8 times, k2. 28 sts

Row 13: K2, [k1, k2tog] 8 times, k2. 20 sts

Row 15: K2, [k2tog] 8 times, k2. 12 sts

Row 16: [P2tog] 6 times. 6 sts

Break yarn and thread through rem. sts. Pull tight and fasten. Sew diagonally across the head of the pixie using running sts.

Hair style 1: Bunches

Cut 30 strands of Crepe measuring 20 cm (8 in). Fold a strand of hair in half, insert the crochet hook into the edge of the hair cap, hook the middle of the strand over the hook, pull back and then insert both ends of the strand through the loop created. Pull tight to secure. Continue to do this all along the edge of the hair cap and then along the center of the head. Tie the hair in two bunches on the head and secure with a few sts. Tie two little bows with strands of Fennel.

Hair style 2: Straight

Cut 30 strands of Otter measuring 20 cm (8 in). Place three strands of Otter in the middle of the scalp and secure using a backstitch. Repeat along the length of the head. Trim as desired.

Hair style 3: Curly

Wind Jet around a knitting needle and secure. Dampen the yarn and leave it to the side until it's completely dry. Repeat on a second needle. Once the yarn has dried, pull it from the needle. It should now be curly. Without stretching the yarn, cut strands of 20 cm (8 in) in length. Secure to the head as Hair style 2.

# ACKNOWLEDGEMENTS

While writing this book I have often played the role of the ogre, the troll, the wicked witch and the dragon, especially towards my very own knight in shining armor, my very loving husband Craig. You always seem to be able to talk me out of a tantrum when a pattern doesn't want to go the way I want it to or when I need to start all over again on something I had been working on for what seemed like forever.

A special thank you goes to my two little princes, Zander and Taylan, who always give me so much praise and encouragement and brighten up my life every single day. You are my world.

Thank you to my loving family and in-laws for supporting me throughout this project.

I'd also like to thank Helen and Hayley for being the best friends a girl could hope for. You've kept my spirits high and picked me up whenever I stumbled.

Thank you to Diane Ward from New Holland Publishers for believing in me once again. It's been a pleasure to work with you.

A special thanks goes to Elizabeth Pierre for so patiently testing many of the patterns in this book. You're a very talented lady with an amazing eye for detail.

Last but not least I'd like to thank CarolAnn and Thomas B Ramsden & Co (www.tbramsden.co.uk) for so generously providing the yarn support for this book.

First published in 2016 by New Holland Publishers Pty Ltd
London • Sydney • Auckland

The Chandlery Unit 704 50 Westminster Bridge Road London SE1 7QY United Kingdom
1/66 Gibbes Street Chatswood NSW 2067 Australia
5/39 Woodside Ave Northcote, Auckland 0627 New Zealand

www.newhollandpublishers.com

A record of this book is held at the British Library and the National Library of Australia.

ISBN: 9781742577852

Managing Director: Fiona Schultz
Publisher: Diane Ward
Project Editor: Holly Willsher
Designer: Andrew Quinlan
Cover Design: Lorena Susak
Production Director: Olga Dementiev
Photography: Sue Stubbs
Printer: Toppan Leefung Printing Ltd

10 9 8 7 6 5 4 3 2 1

Keep up with New Holland Publishers on Facebook
www.facebook.com/NewHollandPublishers

US: $19.99
UK: £14.99